Feeling Seen

Feeling Seen

RECONNECTING IN A DISCONNECTED WORLD

Jody Carrington, PhD

Collins

HarperCollins Publishers Ltd
Bay Adelaide Centre, East Tower
22 Adelaide Street West, 41st Floor
Toronto, Ontario, Canada
M5H 4E3

www.harpercollins.ca

Library and Archives Canada Cataloguing in Publication

Title: Feeling seen : reconnecting in a disconnected world / Jody Carrington, PhD.
Names: Carrington, Jody, author.
Description: Includes bibliographical references and index.
Identifiers: Canadiana (print) 20220428476 | Canadiana (ebook) 20220428514
ISBN 9781443466929 (softcover) | ISBN 9781443466936 (EPUB)
Subjects: LCSH: Social interaction. | LCSH: Social isolation. | LCSH: Social participation. | LCSH: Interpersonal relations.
Classification: LCC HM1111 .C37 2023 | DDC 302—dc239

Printed and bound in the United States of America
23 24 25 26 27 LBC 7 6 5 4 3

These words were created for you on Treaty 7 land, also known as the central part of the Province of Alberta, Canada. It is the home of the Blackfoot Confederacy, including Siksika (Sick-sick-ah), Piikani (Pee-can-ee), and Kainai (Kigh-a-nigh), the Tsuut'ina (Soot- ina [a bit of a stop after the t]) Nation and Stoney Nakoda First Nations, as well as the Métis Nation Region Three.

It is my honor, but mostly my privilege, to live here, create here, and raise my babies here, on a land where so much sacrifice was made. I started on the proverbial third base, and I hope to never, ever forget that my job is to acknowledge, for the rest of my days, just what it means to have this privilege. With this privilege comes the lifelong responsibility to engage in reconciliation efforts: to learn, unlearn, and act in ways that are better than many who have come before me. Always, and in all ways, I will strive to use my privilege to raise the voices that have been silenced for so long.

To all the ones walking me home—feeling seen by you and you feeling seen by me is the only thing that matters in the end. I will always, in all ways, do the thing that I think will make you the proudest. To my A+a+e+a, Mom and Dad, Curt and Val, and my insightful, dedicated, brilliant, kind/no-bullshit team, these words are for you.

CONTENTS

BEFORE WE DIVE IN

You'll notice strong words on some pages and the occasional use of profanity—my authentic self comes with an uncensored-language version that will shine through when a thought or an opinion needs to be accentuated. My intention is never to offend. My intention is to draw attention to some truths I think are long overdue for serious consideration and light. Sometimes we need more emphasis than an "oh, shoot" or "this is so darn hard" when we are talking about life-threatening, life-altering issues. So, if you're up for the challenge, let's fucking dance.

Feeling Seen

The Universal, Possessed-by-All-Mastered-by-None Answer to It All

We look all the time, but we don't see. We listen, but we don't hear. In this world where there is so much noise, we've been missing, more and more these days, the thing that matters most: We were never meant to do any of this alone. I remember where I was standing when this knowing sunk into my soul—as both the biggest reason for such pain in this world and the solution to it all—we just want to feel seen. In the history of our lives, however, we've never been more disconnected, more unseen, as a globe, than we are right now. Bold statement, I know. But I mean it.

You know those moments when you read or hear words or music and, even if for just a few seconds, something seems to shift? Suddenly, there's a moment of clarity? Many have names for these experiences that change the course of everything—Oprah's "aha moments," perhaps. Or the theologian's "Great Epiphany" or a sit-down-leave-it-all-on-the-table "come to Jesus." So let's jump right in with the boldest, most audacious thesis I wish the helpers and the hurt among us knew: The answer to the world's most significant human-centered problems is simply this: We all just want to feel seen. Then, and only then, will we rise. This concept might be captured most eloquently in the words of a hockey coach I knew who said, "You should see how fast I can get a kid to skate when I know the name of his dog."

To be clear, "looking and seeing" often has nothing to do with eyesight—think of it more as a feeling. Feeling seen is something that is heard by the deaf and felt by the blind. It's a universal, unifying experience—it pays no mind to age, race, religion, socio-economic status, physical ability, or gender identity. It's something that is possessed by all of us, yet it is mastered by none. If done genuinely, it rarely gets old. It's like fuel for the strength needed to navigate our days. I truly hope the answer—or some answers—to "it all" lies in the words you'll find here. In these pages, we'll journey through three parts as I

1. share how I think we got so lost and disconnected in this human experience;
2. give you a roadmap to find our way back to each other; and
3. leave you with three practices I think you can always reconnect to when (not if) you lose your way again.

As a clinical psychologist who sits with people who are often struggling with relationships in one way or another, it still amazes me that the hardest thing you and I will ever do is look, genuinely, at the people we care about. It takes as much to give it away as it does to receive the experience of truly "seeing" another. And it's so much easier, and certainly so much safer, to stay distracted with our busy lives and simply look away. Ironically, it's seeing the meaningful relationships that we have with one another that can be the healthiest part of any human life. Relationships seem also the thing that leave so many of us fucked up. Even though we would die as infants without them—we are biologically wired for connection—the same entity (an interaction between two people) is the cause of the most unthinkable trauma. And in another twist of irony, it's only in relationships that we heal those most devastating experiences. Although many would identify "family, my kids, my spouse, my closest friends" as the most important to each of us, it never escapes me just how difficult it is to look into the eyes of the people we love. And it seems, as this world turns and becomes more divisive, as the physical proximity between us continues to expand, as technological advances make it less necessary to be together, this critical dance of relationships—how we interact and communicate—is only becoming more complex, more isolated.

So much has changed within our lifetimes, yet so much of how we interact with each other has not been rewritten. We're doing what we've always done in relationships because, well, it's always been done this way. In fact, many "best practices" we employ to interact with each other were created for a world that no longer exists. And the evidence that we simply cannot do things effectively in a disconnected world? The cost? A mental health pandemic. A rise in divorce, domestic violence, depression, loneliness, anxiety, and war. In fact, it has become an epidemic, this disconnection thing, and it just may require a revolutionary effort to get us to truly look at and see each other. A reconnection revolution. A call for simply connecting is no longer enough. Although connection is what we're wired for, it's the easy part. The hard part comes when our ability to reconnect is required to repair or re-engage, especially after we've been wronged, marginalized, alienated, or hurt. To see and be seen again is then especially risky.

I spend a lot of time thinking about how much I wish people knew just how much they mattered to each other. About how many times just a smile, or a kind gesture, not only changed a life, but saved it. In your least special, or educated, or curated moments, you are woven into the memories that so many hold dear. If you only knew. And here's the reason for these words on these pages. What if you did? What if you knew? Could you hold a gaze a little longer? Could you find grace a little easier? Just imagine with me, even for a moment, what that might mean. In this disconnected world, the answers to reconnection are not something new we have to learn. They are simply getting back to what we've always known when we slow down, drop our shoulders, and remember why we're here. How have we gotten so far away from this in our families, our friendships, our communities, our organizations, you ask? So many little things have added up to so much disconnect. And it's the little things, reminding each of us, one by one, that we have everything we need, right here, right now, to reconnect and bring us back home.

The problem is, we're fucking tired. All the yoga, kale, and getting your water in doesn't address what we are wired for: connection. To other people. So the answer, in fact, does indeed start within us. Not with just the bullshit "self-care" strategies, but with the simple understanding and acknowledgment of just how much it takes to show up for each other. My hope is that these words will stand the test of time because we will never outgrow or automate this process of seeing and feeling seen. It will take practice. And you'll get good at this process the more you repeat it.

I will tell you from the bottom of my soul that this is the book I need to read, too. I want these words to be something I can revisit when, not if, I retreat to the safety of not seeing people, especially the ones who need it the most. Turns out, they're the hardest to give it to. When you are acknowledged, you will rise. And so many of us—if we only knew—are needed to rise in this moment. Needed to deeply feel all of it: love, happiness, grief, fear, anger, and hope. Needed to feel seen, now more than ever. In fact, our next generations depend on it.

Rarely does one thinker's thoughts ever represent their own. Over my almost 20-year career, I have read and listened to the words of many others. And that's the way I prepare to write by thinking about how those words make sense in my head and in my experience. You'll see many incredible souls and their works reflected here. You will also see what it looks like to live out my understandings in my marriage, in my role as a mom to our three babes, and then in my position as a leader (and learner) in this group of amazing humans we call Carrington & Company. The thoughts that come together in these pages are from comments and musings and conversations over wine and (edited) experiences within the therapeutic context where I have heard so many stories of soul-ripping relationships that have disintegrated. Also noteworthy is that although I have attempted to bring light to the complexities of cultural differences that show up in all our relationships, I've interpreted all this through my white, cisgender, able-bodied lens and I know that even on my best days, I have so much left to see in others.

RECONNECTING THE DISCONNECTIONS STARTS IN THE TELLING OF OUR STORIES

First, a story-time segue. Bit early for a segue maybe, but there's something to this concept of storytelling that allows the things that happen in our lives to make the most sense. The words of Indigenous leader, author, and storyteller Richard Wagamese reminded me that, in fact:

All that we are is story. From the moment we are born to the time we continue on our spirit journey, we are involved in the creation of the story of our time here. It is what we arrive with. It is all we leave behind. We are not the things we accumulate. We are not the things we deem important. We are story. All of us. What comes to matter then is the creation of the best possible story we can while we're here; you, me, us, together. When we can do that and we take time to share those stories with each other, we get bigger inside, we see each other, we recognize our kinship—we change the world, one story at a time . . .

I think, in the mix of emotion and memories, the best any of us can do is tell our own story, our own truth. It's often simply in the telling of the story that healing happens. Telling stories is an ancient spiritual practice, a tool for communication, and a way of passing on experiences through generations. See, the human brain has been on a slower evolutionary trajectory than the techno-logical advances we've been making, particularly in the past two generations. Our brains still respond to content by looking for the story to make sense out of the experience. No matter how fast technology can assist with processing data, the meaning starts in the brain. Stories act as the vehicles that, by stimulating neural pathways, trigger our imagination. By engaging our imagination, we become participants in the narrative and can make sense of things differently or deepen an experience.[1]

It's hard when you want to tell your story, I've discovered, because there's a necessary connection between all of us that then makes everyone else's story a part of yours. How do I tell mine without assuming the role of others? Or without talking about a mom or a dad or a sister or a brother in a way that isn't accurate or may even be hurtful? How do you speak your truth if someone else might not even know theirs? It's the tricky part about stories, you see—because what's true for you might not be true for someone else, even if you lived within the same chapters. In fact, I think it is this fear that often prevents many of us from telling our story.

It seems to me, however, that we must put all the pieces on the table somewhere—at least the ones we know—if we want accurate understandings of ourselves. Then, as we start talking, sometimes pieces we didn't even know were there start to emerge. Seeing your story in print or sharing it with another is the critical part. And then integrating and reconnecting those pieces allows for growth, and openness, and freedom.

A PIECE OF MY STORY

My story, just like yours, has changed over the years as I learn about new pieces, gain new perspectives and insights, and develop more words for experiences I didn't know how to talk about.

I think that's where we'll really start—with a bit of my story as it stands true today. I didn't have to go too far back to understand why reconnection and feeling seen matters so much to me. In fact, disconnection was a part of my story even before I was born—although I didn't know about it until I was 36. I think these disconnections played a role in my becoming a psychologist, although at the time I didn't know that either—until some of these pieces started to come together.

A big part of my story begins in a small farming town where I, a white-privileged kid, grew up with a lot: many people who loved me, safety, and routine. Even within this pretty picture, I have a clear memory of the first time I realized my role was to fill in the empty spaces. It's fuzzy now. Whether I'm telling the story about a photograph or if I actually remember it, I'm not really sure. But I know it was a birthday party. We were in the double-wide trailer where we lived until I was 11, but I was about six in this memory. It was summertime. I remember being the fat kid. Permed hair. And somehow being very clear that it was my responsibility to make people laugh. Somehow, I felt it was my job to protect them all—this family of mine (I was the oldest grandchild on both sides)—with humor. With loud distraction. With joy. Maybe I've made that up, knowing what I know now, but I always felt that, more than anyone else, I needed to make them laugh. To this day, I am often the most fulfilled when I can make that mama of mine laugh or get my dad enthralled in a sarcastic rally of the wits. My dad—he was, is—so funny, too. But always on the surface—never too deep. Those deep emotions were always off limits. The emotional stuff was Mom's lane. And she took it on as a job. But I understand now, so much more deeply, I think, why delving into emotions for Dad might have been more difficult. And why, maybe, my mom has so many emotions right on the surface and why I always loved it the most when I could make them both just laugh.

Here are the facts: My parents, who were high school sweethearts, got pregnant in their teens. There was some time before Mom knew she was carrying a baby. Pregnancy tests were not a thing. You had to go to the doctor to get that confirmed. This young woman, my mom, was wildly committed to not disappointing her hard-working, religious parents and she very much respected my dad's parents—also very devoted and rule-bound souls (my grandmother in particular). As I understand it today, my mom and dad had a conversation, many conversations, perhaps, and agreed they would do everything they could to not break the hearts of their parents. So they chose to keep the pregnancy a secret. From everyone. My dad somehow found a "home for unwed mothers" in a city five hours away. They, my pregnant teenaged mom and my dad spun a story that my mother was going to take a job in the next province and my father was going to drive her there. Their parents bought it, apparently—it helped that there were no easily accessible phones or vehicles—Dad was able to get Mom there safely, where she spent the last almost two months of her pregnancy. Alone.

I have very few details of what that stay was like for my mother and even fewer about how my dad handled his emotions. We've talked about it in pieces over the years. Mom and I even drove to the place where she believes she was housed during her pregnancy. Just bearing witness to those memories has, to this point, been difficult to hold as her daughter. I still can't believe that for 40 years, no one other than my mom, not one person, knew what those days and weeks were like for her. And no doubt, equally excruciating but with even less of a place to put his emotions, my father waited for the call to come and get her.

My sister, who my mom named Kimberley Ann at birth, was born that December, via C-section. I have since learned that many babies delivered who were to be "put up" for adoption arrived via C-section, with the thought that it was part a scheduling convenience for the doctor. But also, the scar would serve as a shameful lesson to the mother of her ungodly choices. Kimberley Ann was adopted by a beautiful family six weeks later. She has a mom and a dad who named her Valerie. She has a brother and a large extended family who love her dearly. She later discovered, in a conversation with her mom, that she became very ill with pneumonia in those first few weeks when she was alone before she was adopted. There's something about that part of her story that leaves me with the biggest ache in my heart. I hope there was someone there to rock her. It wasn't my mom—she was only allowed to hold her daughter for 20 painful minutes, while she wept, because the nurses said that the baby's head was slightly misshapen at birth. My mother remembers screaming a demand to simply see her girl, ever so briefly, saying, "I just desperately need to know she is okay." The nurses, she remembers, reluctantly allowed it to calm my hysterical mother. She wailed, my mother did, as they took her baby away, believing she would never see her again.

After a few days to allow my mother to recover, my father came to retrieve my mom and they drove back home to their small town, with the story that Mom's job didn't work out. Neither of them ever told a soul about their firstborn for 38 years. There was very little language between the two of them that would have allowed for the enormity of the emotions. Neither of them recalls ever speaking about her for fear of the repercussions.

My parents got married a few years later but agreed they could not look for their daughter. Even to this day, both my parents are adamant they could not have told their families. There was no emotional language, as teenagers, to address this experience, and so it stayed, for years, unattended to. And as I think about that, in this moment, I am simply attempting to hold space for what that would have been like as a young couple, marrying with such a huge secret. What did it feel like to simply look at each other? I'm imagining they couldn't bear it for long. They didn't want to disrupt the life that her adoptive parents were (they hoped) creating for her. They requested that she be raised in the Ukrainian and Catholic traditions, but they were clearly and adamantly told at the home that they could never look for her.

Now, here comes my favorite part of the story—where I come in. My parents had me in 1975 and my brother Curtis in 1978. They separated briefly in 1987. I don't remember a disagreement between them, let alone a fight, but there was an undeniable chasm that no one else knew about, and which neither of them could talk about.

They did their ever best, as I understand now, to sidestep this big hole, no doubt with a disconnect between them that even they didn't understand. They divorced in 1994.

Years later, when I turned 36, married and pregnant with my own first child, my mom called to ask if I could come home to the farm for the weekend. This wasn't out of the norm. My husband was in Texas that weekend, judging cattle, so it seemed like the perfect weekend to soak up some family time. It was a Saturday morning in January. My parents had been divorced for many years at this point, each with a new partner. My brother still lived close (up the road, in fact), with two daughters. Mom and I were having a coffee when Dad and my brother just walked in. Although Mom and Dad remained cordial with each other, it was weird, I thought, that Dad would just walk in and pull up a chair at the kitchen table. There we were, the four of us, seated at the same spots we claimed many years ago, before the divorce. I remember Mom brought over the lemon loaf (the universal sign of death). And then Dad said these words: "Kids, there's something we need to tell you." Then he started to cry. And Mom started to cry. I looked at my brother to see if this was some sort of fucked-up intervention, but he clearly was as stunned as I was. I instantly assumed one of them was dying and I quickly calculated how long they would have to stay alive to meet my unborn child (it's always about me). Then Dad said, "We have to tell you something that we haven't told anyone in 40 years."

Can I just tell you—I clearly remember the relief I felt. No one was dying. The next sentence, however, was something I would have never guessed, even if you had given me a million chances. He said, "Your mother and I got pregnant when we were very young, and you have a sister." A what? I was okay up until this point, to be honest, and then the heavy comes in. Dad is blathering on about the fact that she's amazing, "she looks just like your mom, she is so much like you, Jod." I remember asking, incredulously, "You've *met* her?" Dad said, "Yes, we have. Separately." And then the big kicker: "Kids, would you like to meet her?" Whoa! Hold up. Thirty seconds ago, I was the oldest and the only daughter. Now I'm the middle kid? And you want us to meet her? As I was contemplating the days, weeks, maybe even months of preparation it might take for me to be ready for the big reveal, my brother pipes in, "Of course, Dad, Mom. We would love to meet her." Jesus. What is even happening here?

And then Dad says, "Great! She's in the garage." Like a fucking puppy!

To be honest, I have a flair for the dramatic, and I've always told the story like this. The truth is, she was on her way to the farm in her car and she had given our parents the direction that if either Curt or I weren't "ready" to meet her, they would text her and she'd turn the car around. Let me tell you—I seriously considered playing the "I'm not ready" card. But come on. There's another one of us? A full biological other one of us? I needed to get a look at this. So, within 15 minutes, my brother and I were watching her drive up our childhood driveway. Curtis and I were holding hands (which is weird for us), and I remember asking him, "What the fuck are you supposed to say to a sister?" And he said to me, "I don't know, Jod. Let's start with hello." And suddenly, there she was. In our kitchen. We said, "hello," and I simply couldn't look away from the most profound piece of my story that I never even knew existed.

She's beautiful. And kind. And funny. And older. Turns out, we grew up one hour from each other. (Did we ever run into each other?) She has a degree in psychology, married a firefighter, and has a son who looks more like me than my own sons do. And she feels like home. Mostly, I'm grateful that she worked so hard to find us. And reconnect the disconnected parts that had lived so long in my mom and in my dad.

There are so many stories in there that aren't mine to tell. Like what this meant for my brother, my dad, my mom. And what about their moms and dads—my grandparents? Even though we considered ourselves a very connected family, all four of my grandparents went to their graves not knowing of their eldest granddaughter. And, of course, what this all means for my sister. And her mom, and her dad, and her brother. What it means to love and raise a child as your own, and always wonder if they, or you, would meet the group of people who share their DNA. Do you love them? Do you hate them? What if you lose the one you raised back to them?

Part of what we'll talk about in this book is simply being aware of all the emotions that are inherently mixed up in this thing we call life—for each of us. Not feeling, if even briefly, the hardest parts of our stories will inevitably make it more difficult to see and be seen. Family systems, emotional relationships, are so different across race and culture, and the dynamics fascinate me, for sure. I will reference some of those differences throughout these pages. However, our most significant focus will be on the need to feel seen, which remains the most profoundly universal desire.

We will navigate these chapters together—how we got so lost, how we find our way back to each other, and what to do *when* (not *if*) we lose our way again. We will walk through research and clinical stories with purpose as we talk about emotions and how they shape the relationships we're in. Each chapter will have a "bring it back home" section to ground us. Along with having big discussions about hard things, we must hold space for big emotions.

Putting the pieces together has allowed me to write these next chapters in my own story with conviction. With an appreciation and empathy for so many of us, all of us, in fact, who have so many seasons of disconnection. What I've learned thus far, dear ones, is that authentic reconnection to your own story first, and then to the people who are walking alongside you, will remain the reason we're all here. We all have the capacity to look and see the people we love and lead. However, it's often so much easier not to look. And although sometimes this avoidance is protective and even necessary, there is a cost to it. Mostly, the less practice we get at truly and authentically connecting and reconnecting to each other, the less skilled we, and the children who come after us, will become.

In all the relationships you are navigating within and around you, in this moment, just know that you matter to so many of the players, especially the ones who may be the hardest to connect with. If we only knew the depths of our influence and just how much our people need to feel seen, I think we would lean further into our relationships. Hence, the stories and the research gathered within these pages are meant simply to do one thing: reconnect us all in this disconnected world.

Part One

HOW WE GOT SO LOST

THE SOUL-RIPPING CONTRIBUTIONS
TO A DISCONNECTED WORLD

"Relationship" is a single word that carries with it the complexities of the world. Although unique to different cultures across this globe, the importance of connection to the people we walk through this life with transcends age, race, religion, socioeconomic status, and gender identity. Feeling seen always happens in the context of a relationship, and an emotional language is the glue that holds it all together. Every single one of us has many relationships to varying degrees of complexity. In fact, the words of the great psychologist Esther Perel echo as mantras to everyone I've ever sat with in my office: "It is the quality of your relationships which ultimately will determine the quality of your life."[1] Our job is to write them well and edit them often. The one thing I can tell you I have felt almost every day of my career is that I wish the people who have sat across from me knew just how powerful they are in the relationships that have left them broken, or sad, or hopeless. In fact, in my office, the words of philosopher and yogi Ram Dass hang over my shoulder; his words have profoundly impacted the way I think about everything in this life. He said, "We're all just walking each other home."[2] So much of my work is simply to hold space and remind people that we are all just walkers for each other. The connections among us are necessary for survival. Yet it seems to me that, in the

17

history of the world, we have never been more disconnected than we are right now. Most every issue anyone has carried into my office has something to do with the often huge disconnect between intention and perception that always gets mixed up in this human relationship thing. Hurt and pain quickly (understandably) turn to armor—and relationships suffer. People stop feeling seen (and sometimes never truly were seen in the first place). This can happen over years of disconnect that slowly erode relationships—or it can happen in a sudden, severing blow.

In fact, let me take you into my office. Picture it. Someone is seated by the window, turned at a slight angle toward me. I'm seated in my regular spot, in a brown leather swivel chair. We both have coffee mugs perched on the table between us—often untouched following the first few sips. After we spend a while understanding all the things weighing heavy on their mind, I ask them some sort of question that sounds like "Where in your body do you feel it?" Sometimes there's resistance to this question. ("What do you mean, where do I feel it?") Other times, it's answered immediately. The feeling usually lands somewhere in the core—most often in the chest, sometimes the shoulders, the neck, or the pit of the stomach. Turns out, most of our biggest experiences get stored somewhere in our body—described beautifully by the title of trauma expert Bessel van der Kolk's book, *The Body Keeps the Score*.[3]

I always like to know if that "feeling" lodged in the chest, neck, or pit of the stomach has a shape or a color. Some have described that feeling as "a heavy, silver-plated ball"; or "it's like a sharp-edged orange fiery triangle"; or just "a blob of nothing." When people describe these things, they sometimes also have a sense that the feeling is heavy, and it's been there a long time. Often, this feeling (that is now a shape) is unwanted or even feared. There's usually a visceral reaction to these heavy senses that have grown into the very being of people just like you and me, who are desperate to have "it"—that feeling—identified. And, most importantly, fixed or removed.

This is where the remarkable part comes in. I often ask, "What happens to that entity when we just notice it? Acknowledge it? Even welcome it?" To wonder, in fact, if that thing could have been there for so long because at one time it served a purpose. Just notice what happens when we tell it, gently or firmly, that it doesn't need to go anywhere. Today, we are just witnessing it.

And you know what happens—every time? This entity, this block, this heavy weight starts to shift, at worst. And at best, it starts to fade or shrink and become less of a burden. (That's when the real shifts start to happen.) There's so much within that shape that carries the interpretation of a story and what it meant at the time. And, of course, it's different for everyone—and that's the fun part for me. Often, that shape or feeling needs simply to be witnessed. See, there's a power in the telling, and retelling, of our own stories that I don't think we even understand the magnitude of. Naming it to tame it[4] is powerful because those emotions you own can be unruly. In fact, words are necessary for us tellers of our own stories to say, in order to write our next chapters. Necessary to create understandings and to weave together the broken pieces as legacies that each of us will leave.

Becoming increasingly disconnected, over multiple generations, means that so many emotions and feelings have been left unwitnessed. And pain and disconnection have followed. The first part of this book will be a critical look at some of the contributors to how we got so lost and disconnected. It will likely be, for most of you, the heaviest part of this book. We could easily just jump to how we fix it all, but believe me when I say this: You can't address what you don't acknowledge. So let's gently, but with conviction, unpack some of the things that are adding to the disconnect many of us are mired in. Buckle up.

CHAPTER ONE

Emotional Dysregulation

EVERYONE'S LOSING THEIR FRIGGIN' MIND

A s a psychologist, I have long had a thing for relationships and the emotions that live within them. Let me be clear: other people's relationships and emotions. Knowing how critical the whole talking and bringing darkness into the light thing is, it still doesn't come easy when it's about the emotions I personally need to call into awareness or be responsible for. I'm not a fan, really. I also know this to be true: Those who are the most connected among us are better at feeling. It's a complex paradox of a process, turns out, this feeling thing. Emotions can change on a dime, take you to the highest highs and drop you to your knees. It is, in fact, one of the many things that make human beings way more alike than different. We all have a complexity of emotions. It's in what we do with those emotions—how we manage them, process them, hold them, or push them away—that often determines just how authentically we're available to engage with those around us.

We tend to be the calmest and most connected emotionally when we are looking at and truly seeing another. It requires a regulated focus and stability to bear witness to another. The opposite is more often experienced: the rush and hurry of our day; the just hoping that "this too will pass." Brushing by or stuffing emotions can sometimes be the only thing we have time for. Yet in this culture we put a strong emphasis on that calmness. We like it best when those around us are calm, connected, using their words. It's when we fall in love the deepest. It's when we think the clearest. It's when we process or come to terms the best. We don't like it much when others are messy, dysregulated, or disconnected.

Although I've been in this business of emotions for a while, there is still one single concept that has completely changed the game for me. I don't remember learning it in grad school—although I'm sure we did, among all the lessons of the tried-and-true behaviorism. It wasn't until I landed my first real job, on the psychiatric inpatient unit of a children's hospital, immersed in looking at relationships through a trauma-informed lens, that I truly understood the power of the two words that have since defined my understanding of, well, everything: *emotional regulation*. I would confidently argue that at the heart of all physical and mental health is one's ability to emotionally regulate. I wish I'd learned it earlier in my career, but I can tell you that understanding just what emotional regulation means has changed my life, not only as clinician but also as a wife, as a mom, and as a friend and a leader.

THE REGULATING OF THOSE UNRULY EMOTIONS

Emotional regulation is the ability to stay calm in times of distress. See, when you have the ability to *not* lose your friggin' mind when things get rough, overwhelming, or difficult, you tend to do better in this world. You have access to emotions and to where "making sense of it all" lives. Turns out, none of us are born with the skills to regulate emotion well. When babies come home from the hospital, how do they let you know what they need? They cry. They lose their friggin' minds. And what do we big people typically and instinctually do with a crying infant? We soothe them. We attempt to regulate them. We walk them home. Often, in fact, there's a rhythmic exchange that happens between the infant and the one doing the soothing. And this rhythmic exchange— bouncing, humming, rocking, patting—is a universal experience, transcending culture, age, and gender. This is not a coincidence, but in fact this universal rhythmic exchange between caregivers and children represents one (among many, actually) undeniable, unifying experience that every single soul on this planet shares: the first sound every single one of us feels—the heartbeat of our mother. This visceral, soothing *buhm-buhm, buhm-buhm* becomes the place we either go to internally or seek externally when it all gets too much. We all, essentially, feel it in our bones.

The more often we calmly walk babies through distress by regulating them, the more they eventually become proficient at doing this when there's no one there to help them. The healthiest among us tend to be the ones who were lucky, privileged, blessed enough to have been surrounded by several regulated "walkers"— those who could help us name what we were feeling, not leave us or abandon us when we were distressed. Those who gave us a sense of safety, predictability, and calm more often than not. Having others available to show us how to calm in times of distress allows us first to learn the skill of emotional regulation and then, eventually, to learn how to show others the way. If that didn't happen for you, if many of the big people in your world struggled with their own ability to regulate, or weren't (or couldn't be) present because of their own trauma, or frequently told you to "shut up" or said "you're an idiot," you may not have been shown, consistently or effectively enough, how to calm in times of distress. Further, if you were raised in a gender-typical environment—like many of us were, including me—we learned early that "boys don't cry" and, mostly, it's better to be "tough" than to show emotion. There's a perpetuated system where girls are given many opportunities to be shown how to regulate, while we prefer that boys just "suck it up." We will talk much more about this in the pages that follow. For now, the issue is: You need to make space for big emotions if you ever hope to address them. And you can't give away something you've never or rarely received.

WE NEVER OUTGROW IT

And here's the other interesting part: We never outgrow this need to have another person walk us through the hard things. When we lose our minds with any big emotion, including joy, or fear, or overwhelm, we generally navigate those experiences so much better if there's someone who can share it with us. Just think about the last time something "big" happened to you that was accompanied by a big rush of emotion. Like learning you're pregnant, getting in a car accident, or hearing the words "it's cancer." It's rare that when big, emotional experiences cross our path on any given day, we don't need (sometimes desperately) to seek another who can share in that emotion and, often, help us make sense of it all. And see, we tend to be quite selective about who we choose to do this walking—if we're lucky enough to have choices. For example, as I drove to a talk one snowy morning in a city I was unfamiliar with, I looked down at the navigation system—and rear-ended the van ahead of me. My seatbelt locked as I was slammed forward with the sudden impact and, instantly, my heart started racing. I heard myself saying "no, no, no" (and no doubt a few other choice words that started with f). As I focused on the vehicle I had hit, I saw the outline of three car seats in the back row of the van and nearly threw up. Being in an accident was one thing, but an accident with a car full of babies was another.

I pulled over, as did the woman I hit. She was out of her vehicle even before I could open my door, and I heard myself apologizing before my feet hit the snowy pavement. She was visibly shaken, not happy to see me, and was opening the van door to check on her children. The babies were scared but okay, and I watched this mama masterfully reassure and regulate them. We exchanged our information after assessing that both vehicles were drivable. (And I learned a lot about that amazing mama in those brief few moments on the side of the road.) As soon as I got back into my car, however, the emotions came fast and furious, angst accompanied by tears. My first call was to my husband; he's generally the go-to in times of big emotion. That was my second mistake of the day. As soon as he heard my voice, he asked anxiously, "What's wrong?" I told him. His very next question, I swear to God, was "Is the vehicle okay?" In his defense, his response may have been instinct, or maybe the way I sounded in those first few seconds just made him believe I was okay. But I spit back, "Yes. The vehicle is fine. And so is the mother of your three children. Except for my heart, which I need someone to hold right now, and that someone does not appear to be you." And I hung up and called my sister. Now even as I write this, I understand it sounds a bit harsh. But seriously? Is the car okay? Fuck right off. I have very little access to my prefrontal cortex right now and I just need someone who can walk me home before we start talking about insurance claims. Got it?

My sister was just what I needed, calm and steady. The first words out of her mouth were "It's just a vehicle, my girl. The most important thing is that you're okay. Where are you, because I'm on my way." My heart was already slowing down, and it didn't take long until we had made sense of it all. Having someone who is calm (at least calmer than ourselves) to collect our emotions (not try to fix them) is all we need in those moments. Sometimes, the ones we choose will be different, depending on the circumstance, but if there's someone who can hold our hearts when things get rough, we have a much better shot at navigating those experiences and integrating them successfully (and often more quickly).

I will also tell you that when we don't have someone familiar to fall into—when we don't have a choice—we are stripped back to the bareness that is humanity. Some of the most heartfelt stories I've ever heard are those that arise in a crisis when strangers have been left no choice but to instantly lean on each other. There are numerous beautiful stories of connection in some of our most significant global tragedies—stories of people who willingly, gladly, gave up their food, their homes, their resources in time of war, natural disaster, or historic events like the September 11 bombing of the World Trade Center. The faith in humanity is often restored in times of crisis because so many of us would do anything for anybody when we're the ones who are regulated and a fellow human is in need. Especially when we feel like what we do makes a difference. And, for the record, what we do in times of service is rarely forgotten.

HOW THESE EMOTIONS WORK

Let's start with a rudimentary tour through the neurological process of emotion and emotional regulation (I'll make it more fun than it sounds.) Although I learned about the complexities of the brain from several different perspectives in the run of this career, the one (and only) theory that made emotions and the brain clear to me was proposed by Dan Siegel, psychiatrist and brain expert extraordinaire. He calls emotional dysregulation the "lid flip."[1] So, let me take you through the lid flip, as I've made sense of it over the years. For the ease of clarifying the complex process of the brain, think of it as being modeled on the outside of your body by your hand and your arm. Hold up your hand for me right now, with your palm in front of your face, then tuck your thumb on the inside of your palm and wrap your fingers around the outside of your thumb. That, right there, is a hand model of your brain. Your arm represents your spinal cord; your wrist represents your brainstem. Now, I want you to flip those fingers up and notice that your thumb, tucked still on top of your palm, represents your limbic system. All humans develop from the inside out; the most primitive parts are developed first. That thumb (your limbic system) is where your most primitive responses to big emotion live. When we're in a heightened state of arousal, the body enters a biologically protective state and we are left with three primitive emotional regulation strategies, the ones all mammals come hardwired with—"fight, flight, and freeze."[2] Our senses are heightened, and we cut out any of the "extras." We pay less attention to detail and use every bit of our energy searching for danger and reacting to the things that are most concerning. We forgo the many things we have space to attend to when we're relaxed and calm—like the details of a day, where we put our phone, or the beauty of a sunset. It is the place we go when the most instinctual emotions need to take over.

Now I want you to wrap your fingers back around your thumb. Your fingers on our hand model of the brain represent your prefrontal cortex. If our hand model of your brain was currently sitting in your skull, your prefrontal cortex (those four fingers) would live right above your eyes. Your fingers/prefrontal cortex houses everything you've ever learned in your life. Things like your father's middle name, the birth dates of your children, how to dance, the PIN for your bank card, any of the languages you've learned. The things that make us human live there. So do your most important skills, if you've been shown how to do them—things like empathy, kindness, and compassion. See, you're not born with those things. Someone has had to show you or provide that experience. Then, and only then, are you able to give things like empathy or compassion away. So, in my interpretations of Dan Siegel's words, I want you to imagine that your four fingers, that prefrontal cortex, represents a lid. When that lid is wrapped around your thumb, it is "on." Your brain is calm and connected, and you have access to everything you've ever learned. You can use your words, you can remember things easily, and you can feel all the emotions—like empathy, kindness, and compassion—you've ever been taught.

Now consider this: Have you ever heard the expressions "They've flipped their lid! Lost their friggin' mind!"? Primitively speaking, we flip our lids (flip those fingers up and away from the thumb—if you're still playing along) when we're scared or in danger. I mean, it makes sense to me because if you were out frolicking in a park and a huge, aggressive barking dog lunges toward you from out of the bushes, you wouldn't need access to everything you've ever learned in your life. In that moment, you don't need to remember the middle name of your mother or your anniversary date or even the language needed to describe the emotion you're feeling. In that exact moment, you want to flip all those things out of the way and have the brain primitively take over into either fight, flight, or freeze. Likely, in that instant, you'll want to run, if you're able to. And see, the brain is such a cool, complex organism that it just does this automatically.

As I'm sure you can appreciate, in the state that Siegel calls a lid flip, you're unteachable. You're not your "best self" because you're working with only the most primitive parts of who you are. And there's a reason for this when there's an actual threat. When you are an infant who has no resources in that prefrontal cortex to solve the problems that you might need to, you flip it out of the way in the hopes somebody with more skill in that moment will walk you through it. In fact, the more times big people are able to regulate in the physical presence of a child, the better that child begins to develop the skills of emotional regulation.[3] Neural pathways are forged, and a script is provided on what you do when big emotion happens. You can imagine that so much of a baby's experience in learning this process depends entirely on the skill level and the state of the people who surround the baby the most. You can't tell a child how to regulate emotion—you must *show* them. In fact, never in the history of the world has telling somebody to "calm down" or "use your words" been effective. I promise you, if you have ever been commanded to "calm down," rarely has your response been, "Oh right, of course! I was a little worked up there. Let me just pull my shit together."

Let me take you through a typical example with kids. I feel lucky that I got to spend many years in my career working with children because they taught me so much about how adults work. Although I now spend most of my time working with organizations filled with adults, everything comes back to the process of emotional regulation. In fact, when the people we love acquire language, we tend to do more telling than showing. We bark commands to our kids or our partners, particularly when we're stressed or "flipped." We say things like "Relax!" or "What is wrong with you?" We get frustrated when the people around us are not regulated or when they "lose it." Often, with kids especially, we attempt to practice emotional regulation skills as a way of preparing them for when big emotions come. This effort, in and of itself, isn't a bad idea; however, the expectation is often that they'll remember these skills when they're dysregulated.

I'll give you an example. Let's say you have a kid named Levi (I love that name). He's a bit of a lid-flipper. Levi's the kid who rarely makes it through birthday parties without getting into a fight. You're often at your wit's end, telling him things like "calm down" and "don't hit people!" You've tried everything with this kid—taken away his iPad, given him the silent treatment, yelled, shown him that his sister (who often makes better choices) gets more rewards than he does, so he should be more like her. Levi's been grounded, and you've tried talking to him about his actions, repeatedly, and you just can't seem to figure out how to help this babe in making "the good choices."

So, you up the ante and pull in external resources. You put Levi in friendship groups, and you spend a significant amount of time teaching him things like how to take deep breaths and write out his feelings. You even practice: "Levi, look at Mom. What are the strategies that you're going to use if you're out on the playground and somebody hits you today?" And Levi looks at you and takes a deep breath, and he says all the right things. "I'm going to use my words. I'm going to find an adult. I'm going to journal. I'm going to take belly breaths." And this beautiful soul grins with pride at all the things he knows to do. You're markedly impressed with his list of strategies (and no doubt with your ability to finally get through to this kid), so you fist bump and tell him to have a good day. Levi skips out the door, and you feel remarkably good about yourself.

And then, 37 seconds later, what happens? You hear a commotion, and you go out into the hallway. And sure as shit, Levi has just leveled his sister after she looked at him "funny." And you haul Levi back into his bedroom and say, "What is wrong with you? We just practiced this. How many times do I have to do this?" And then you start to wonder, "Maybe this kid has ADHD? Maybe I shouldn't have married his father? He's probably the one with the bad genes." But then you watch Levi with your best friend or even your mother and you think, "Why is the kid so much more compliant with someone else?" Your best friend or your mother likely even says things like "He was just fine until you got home." And then you start thinking it's you. Maybe there's something wrong with you? Maybe that kid would be better off with somebody else?

Deep breath. Ahh! The joys of navigating big emotions in little people. Turns out, many times you're doing a beautiful job because, when this kid is calm, he has everything on board that he needs to know. His biggest struggle is being able to have access to it when things get tough. That's when he needs big people (especially the ones who mean the most to them) either to walk him through it in the moment or to take charge and help get his lid back on and try again. That last part, however, is the script I rarely read in parenting manuals or books. And it's the script that is needed across every institution—every organization. It's the script needed on how we should treat our employees or inmates or a student in a classroom. You can't give away something you've never received, and emotional regulation takes practice. The dysregulation is not to be avoided. In fact, the chaos is necessary to learn the calm.

PRIME DYSREGULATION INGREDIENTS

I've noticed over the years that most people, oh—and the person I look at in the mirror everyday—dysregulate to the highest level when three prime ingredients are present: (1) uncertainty; (2) fear; and (3) no end in sight (when it feels like there isn't a plan). Think about a two-year-old in the middle of a meltdown, for example. The same deal applies for adults. If you've ever witnessed (or been in the middle of) a fight in a bar, you're basically an expert. Now, just as an aside, I've been in two bar fights in my life, and I've witnessed my fair share. I cut my teeth (if you will) in a bar called Billy Bob's, back in the day. If you've ever found yourself in a drinking establishment (to have a night out or perhaps to land a partner), you can imagine what most people look like at the beginning of the night out. Dressed nice, smelling pretty good. There's chatting that happens with a particularly smart and kind prospect. Maybe you have a two-step or two (I'm from the farm) out on the dance floor. You might even be considering if this candidate could be worthy enough to bed down for the night (now there's a term for ya) or maybe even take home to introduce to your mama.

Now, what happens if 30 minutes later, that same potential life partner is out in the parking lot of the bar, fixing to pick a fight with another human who they think spilled their drink? Picture it. You might not even recognize this former dance partner in this state (even though you were basically falling in love just minutes ago), who is now ready to take on some other lid-flipper for some obviously very important reason. And a group of friends are holding their party back. Often there are very few formed sentences or even words, their breathing is shallow, and they're unable to respond to much reason. Imagine, just 30 minutes ago you were considering hooking up with this person, who now can't even form words (other than "fuck," maybe). What if you asked the fighter-person to two-step now? See, when someone gets dysregulated, it's not that they lose the skills to be kind, use their words, or even two-step. This person has lost *access* to those skills.

That's what emotional dysregulation can look like and, in either situation (the kid or the bar fighter), we often judge others (and ourselves) when dysregulation is present. Usually, when someone experiences a similar situation, they require someone who can calm or regulate them. Someone who can "walk them home." Someone (or something) who can slow them down, maybe get them away from the situation, decrease the cortisol in their body, and get their prefrontal cortex back online so they have access to all the good things they know to be true. As we'll talk about in later chapters, this whole regulation process is often very difficult to do alone. And in the "good old days," we didn't realize just how much of this connection thing was simply much more readily available.

THE POWER OF PROXIMITY

Co-regulating with another happens most effectively when you're in the same physical space. Although we can calm people over the phone or online, physical proximity to the other is often one of the most powerful tools. We are wired for connection—that will never become automated. And see, we used to have so much more access to this proximity thing—even just two generations ago. I've considered the complexities for a long time, but in the most simplistic terms, when we were developing "best practices" for human behavior, what was built in (and what we didn't know we had to measure) was the relationship that already existed thanks to the greater access to each other. We lived so much closer together and, if we worked outside the home, we worked in smaller buildings. We went to school in smaller institutions. And there was the necessity to speak directly to each other much more frequently. Think about the square footage of the house your grandfather was raised in compared to the square footage of the house where many of us are raising our babies. What's the difference? A significant amount of proximity. I often marveled at my grandparents and their stories. The one-bedroom house my father's parents raised their three boys in. No access to an indoor toilet until my father was 17.

And just two generations ago we had far less access to relational exit ramps. We spent a lot of our spare time with each other, mostly because we didn't have a lot of other options. And in just two generations that has changed significantly, primarily because of technological advances. To love, you must have been loved. The scarcity of relationship interaction is where we see the most dramatic shifts. For example, in a hunter-gatherer clan, the ratio of relationships between adults and children was four to one. Today, the caregiver to children ratio is reversed, one to four. Kids today get about 25 percent of the interactions that kids did if they lived in a hunter-gatherer clan.[4]

Just two generations ago, my grandparents didn't have access to a television and certainly not to a computer or iPad. I remember my grandparents playing a game of cribbage every morning and every night, dealing cards and trading quarters kept in pill bottles. Those were the good old days, they'd say. And when it comes to seeing each other, I tend to agree. Because it was then as it is now; the hardest thing we will ever do is look at the people we love. The more opportunities we have to disengage from each other, turns out, we take them. Technology has made so many of our interactions more efficient, and in a dramatically short period. We will never, however, automate relationships.

ENTER: BEHAVIORISM

With all these emotions just floating around, there has been a long-standing desire to make sense of them. A desire to understand and organize just how we manage these emotions—particularly when they get out of control. In fact, my psychology ancestors tried making sense of this forever. They too were asking: How do we get people to make good choices, stay calm, use their words? As the premise of things, what we started to understand is that you can control behavior by enforcing rules, limits, and boundaries—and particularly effectively if we use pain as a motivator. More specifically, during the first half of the 20th century, John B. Watson developed the theory he called methodological behaviorism.[5] In his theory, Watson understood actions by measuring only observable behaviors and events. In the 1930s, the more insightful B.F. Skinner came along and said, "Wait a second. Thoughts and feelings play a role here, too." He called these insights "radical behaviorism."[6] While Watson and his buddy Ivan Pavlov investigated the stimulus-response procedures of classical conditioning, Skinner assessed the controlling nature of consequences and the mechanisms that signal behavior, calling this process "operant conditioning."[7] Skinner's position (essentially a philosophical one) gained strength with his successful experiments with rats and pigeons that used a lever press to demonstrate just how powerful rewards and consequences can be, even with vermin. Responses are not just reflexes, Skinner discovered. Beings can control behavior.[8]

Basically, these guys tried to make sense of how behavior works by deconstructing it. Which makes sense when you're talking about rats and pigeons. Deconstructing behavior works very well when you don't have a prefrontal cortex in your brain. Humans have one of those. Rats and pigeons do not. Turns out, the prefrontal cortex is an important thing to consider. As parents and teachers, however, we were becoming desperate to make sense of our kids' (unruly) behavior. It appeared to work so well with animals that we decided to adopt the philosophy, and we created numerous parenting programs and education protocols based on what we learned from rats, pigeons, and dogs. It's astounding to think about it. We decided that we should create programs that would "motivate" a kid to be kind or "make good choices." If kids don't make good choices, we punish them until they remember to be kind! Seriously?! I am going to be unkind to you in the hopes you will "snap out of it" and, in the future, do the exact opposite of what I'm doing to you right now. The biggest problem with a strictly behavioral approach is that, in the short term, it works. See, if you have a big enough stick, you can get anyone to comply. The bigger problem, however, is that those best practices for how we view humans were created for a world that no longer exists. When these theories were developed, we had much more access to each other through proximity and relationships. We didn't even know we had to consider or measure those things.

So many of us, you and I both, were raised in this place of strict behaviorism. Kids should be seen and not heard. In fact, this theory is the philosophical foundation of every major institution in our world, including the judicial system, our education system, and many parenting approaches—and, for sure, the way that I was trained as a psychologist not that many years ago. You make a good choice, I support you; you don't make a good choice, I'll punish you or take away things from you until you "learn your lesson." What we didn't ask the rat and the pigeon, however, was how they felt about the folks doing the shocking or considered what skills the shock recipient might have to give away to the next generation.

THE SHACKLES OF SHAME

So much of punishment or consequence has elements of shame and humiliation. We lock people up in jail and take away their clothes, or shun "bad kids" from classrooms or schoolhouses until they can be kind again. The idea, I think, is that these awful feelings will be the motivators to become more like the others, who aren't making such "bad choices." Why do we send kids to their rooms or suspend them? What do we think is going to happen when they're hanging out in these exiled places, often alone?

36

They're just going to have a sudden epiphany and think, "Well, son of a gun. Guess I'm going to try harder to be nicer"? It's so absurd.

Shame is, indeed, one of the most powerful emotions we feel—and, sadly, it doesn't take much to evoke it in another. Particularly if your resources are thin or your confidence is low. These words to describe this emotion make sense to me: "Shame is the fear of disconnection—it's the fear that something we've done or failed to do, an ideal we've not lived up to, or a goal that we've not accomplished makes us unworthy of connection. I'm unlovable. I don't belong."[9] I sat with those words for some time. The fear of disconnection. Of course, connection is so powerful, so much so that we need it like air. We'd forgo relationships if we feel shame. Miss huge opportunities, go broke, risk losing everything, at the expense of shame. Just imagine what happens to your ability to look and see another when you are full of shame.

It's amazing to me that we perpetuate practices within cultures that promote shame and embarrassment, thinking these measures will somehow produce resilient, productive souls who are confident enough to stay connected to another. I have never been surer that, in an organization or system where shame is practiced as a form of behavioral control (e.g., within the justice system, the education system, some farming communities, or sports organizations), the result will not be happy, well people. Further, in some institutions, shame tactics are used as training practices. For example, according to the US Department of Justice, most police recruits receive their training in academies with a stress-based military orientation.[10] These training programs are often modeled after a military boot camp, characterized by paramilitary drills, daily inspections, intense physical demands, public discipline, withholding of privileges, and an immediate reaction to infractions. In fact, the high-stress paramilitary model of training results in police practices that are contrary to democratic and, certainly, empathic considerations. A structure using relationship, experiential learning, and critical thinking would be significantly more effective.[11] We know this to be true. There is essentially no evidence in this generation that those best practices that many of these organizations were built on are supported; and furthermore, they are increasingly harming the emotional culture and subsequent functioning of their employees.

In fact, more shame or humiliation just makes people more ill, resistant, and sometimes even more dangerous. It's often powerful enough to halt an undesirable behavior in the moment, but it doesn't make anyone "learn their lesson" or magically desire to be better. Understandably, shame is highly correlated with addiction and mental health issues like depression and eating disorders.[12] So, pray tell, why do we continue to employ these tactics when shaping the behavior of people we hope will either grow (students), serve (police officers), or heal (prisoners)? While, conversely, "empathy and guilt [in that order] work together to create a force that is both adaptive and powerful."[13] Guilt is often necessary when we've done wrong by another or when we have made a choice that we're disappointed in. Guilt is a much more powerful and adaptive emotion than shame, and far less damaging. Although you can't tell someone how to feel guilt, leading them there is often most swiftly accomplished through empathy.

It has taken me a long time to understand the necessity of the shift to seeing most every behavioral interaction through the eyes of emotional regulation. I've spent a lot of time in my career trying to understand behavior—and not nearly enough time trying to get to the emotion that always (in all ways) drives the behavior. I have a huge understanding of how difficult it will be to begin to think differently, or what it might take to help organizations that have "always done it this way" shift their thinking. I don't think we can tell them; I think we must show them. If we only knew that we have everything we already need, this would, I think, be easier to do than we anticipate. So right now, I believe, more than ever before, we must call for a dramatic paradigm shift. And it starts with you and me.

BRINGING IT BACK HOME

One of the primary contributors to this disconnected world is the difficulty so many of us experience with emotional dysregulation. Think about just how much uncertainty, fear, and the sense of no end in sight has surrounded us, as pandemics, loneliness, wars, and mental health fallouts become more apparent than ever before—not to mention the now-instant access we have to all this data. We have also become more fearful of each other (with legitimate concerns around illness). More importantly, consider the embedded practices of attempting to shame or fix unruly behavior while we have dramatically increased our proximity to and disconnection from each other within just one lifetime. It's become debilitating.

I like the concept of a shift, and I think the time is now. A shift in how we understand each other. So many of those practices are no longer applicable to the way the world is now turning. The time has come, in fact it's probably long overdue, that we start to see each other differently than just by outcomes. What if we started to understand that we are so powerful in support of each other, instead of in competition with each other? Regardless of the unique features we each have, we have this shared responsibility of walking each other home. The heart of all of this, I think, must involve a reconnection with an emotional language. In fact, my wish for this book—and, if I could be so bold, for humanity—is that we will all begin to feel, more deeply and fully, bravely, just one relationship at a time. To start to practice the on-purpose feeling of all the emotions down to our core and understand that indeed there are no bad emotions. As we wrap up this chapter, here are a few things to consider as we bring home this first contributor to the disconnect:

1. Think about your experience with emotional dysregulation in your lifetime. Where have you seen it the most? How was it responded to when it involved you or those around you?

2. When you flip your lid, who has been able to walk you through it? Is there someone you lean on the most to walk you home? Has that changed in the seasons of your life? What did it feel like when someone "got it"? What did it feel like when someone didn't—or they tried to fix it too fast?

3. Consider that emotional regulation is always a skill you can learn—you're never too old to get better at it. When you think about the people in your life, regardless of age, who is the most skilled at staying calm in times of distress in your life?

CHAPTER TWO

No Words

THE LACK OF EMOTIONAL LANGUAGE BETWEEN US

T he primary difference among many of us is what we do with the emotions we are all full of. The more words or expressions you have to communicate within, between, and around your relationships, the healthier you tend to be,[1] most especially when physical closeness to others is unavailable or becomes difficult. Psychologist Susan David talks beautifully about the importance of emotional granularity, accurately putting a name to specific feelings. Remarkably, however, the vast majority of us have access only to the big three emotions: happy, sad, and pissed off.

As I wrote this book, I deliberately tried on emotionally laden words I probably knew existed but hadn't considered in a long time. Words like anguish, tranquility, humiliation, and fervor. Every time I read one of these seemingly brand-new words, I was amazed at the memories they evoked. Turns out, the words used to describe the complexity of emotions we have every day can be vitally important in unlocking how we feel, regulating those feelings, and helping others experience that freedom, too. I am now convinced that our capacity for an emotional language is one of the most important things we need to shift as we move toward reconnecting this world. Could it be that we are more able to truly see each other when we feel more confident in being able to communicate our needs and understand theirs?

Turns out, most of us come with a plethora of emotions somewhere within us. These act as the threads that connect us. So many people have led the way in understanding the power of emotions and how we use them. One of those great teachers, whose work I have carried as a beacon throughout most of my career, is Brené Brown—a social worker, researcher, and storyteller by trade. I sleep with her books on my nightstand and have devoured all the works of the people who have inspired her. In *Atlas of the Heart*,[2] she weaves into our understanding of the English language 87 emotions, suggesting that the ones we have trouble naming, and thus understanding, are often what hold us back. The simplicity of this point never ceases to amaze me: If you have a feeling that you can't identify or name (like the other 84 emotions so many of us feel beyond happy, sad, and pissed off), then this is the place you should start. We do, indeed, need another human who can walk us through feeling all the feelings, or we stay stunted in the basics. If those around us don't talk about feelings, we won't either. And what's most interesting to me these days is that in America, emotional illness—things like post-traumatic stress disorder (PTSD) and depression—is the leading cause of death among us humans, outrunning even cancer at an alarming speed.[3] It is still, sadly, so much more acceptable to have a heart attack than PTSD. But what is becoming more undeniable, perhaps daily, is that emotional illness is demanding our attention and connection. Unacknowledged emotions are more pressing than physical illness. Full stop.

Contrary to popular discussion, emotions are neither universally recognized nor expressed.[4] Context matters significantly.

When you put what is happening in your body into a context, your body makes sense of the feeling. The story you tell about that feeling (e.g., my heart is racing because I'm a failure versus my heart is racing because I'm on a roller coaster) significantly affects how you make sense of that experience. You're not at the mercy of emotions—you have control over them. Your brain is wired so that if you change your ingredients, you can change the emotional responses in your life. Essentially you build your experience by better understanding the interpretation of your responses.[5]

Now, listen: There's a big difference between clinical conditions and simply big emotion. As a psychologist I am very clear that there are emotions that have a neurophysiological component. For some of us, these emotions become debilitating, and that typically leads us into the realm of clinical diagnoses. There are, however, so many more frequent times in our lives when simply understanding our emotions a bit better is the path to freedom from a sometimes remarkable hold. Emotions are built—but not built in.[6] Cultivating our emotions is really at our whim. The key, however, is first being able to identify that those emotions are just that: emotions. They can't keep you, or save you, or free you. They can't kill you. But not talking about them might.

EMOTIONS ARE OUR STRUCTURAL INTEGRITY

Emotions can take time to unpack, and we typically just want to skip to the answers. Just get on with it. Get it done. In fact, so many people enter the therapeutic relationship wanting the answers. I've been asked, often within the first few minutes of a session, "But, what do I do about it"? Or, more typically, "What do I do about them?" I've come to learn (the hard way) that we can't fix what we don't first understand. It's the one thing I think plagues so many of us. Let's get to the answer, give the strategies, just *fix* it—especially

43

when someone (especially ourselves) is distressed or uncomfortable. This is the shittiest part of "the work." It's found in the messiest moments of grief and pain and trauma. And it is necessary to feel it first before we ever attempt to fix it. So, let's first do a deep dive into this emotion thing—most critically, how emotions work and why we're becoming less and less good at them, namely in this current generation. *P.S.: If you're considering just skipping past this section to get to the answer to it all, know that this is likely the part you need to sink into the most.*

UNLOCKING THE SOUL

If we're going to figure this out together, I think we start at the core—from the inside out. It's where we all try to get back to in our clearest moments and, in my humble opinion, a sacred, good place that I think every single human possesses. There have been a lot of descriptors of that holy space—the seed of self, the soul, the source, the center.[7] For the sake of our discussions, let's call this "the soul." Consider this: When our vulnerable souls feel seen, that is what the perfection of the universe looks like. So many of us, however, have made decisions or endured experiences that have created significant armor, barriers, and defenses around that soul, often in an understandable effort to protect it from being hurt. Emotions like shame, abandonment, and jealousy are particularly tough ones that firmly implant themselves and seem impossible to break through. In this journey of walking each other home, and often in my role as a psychologist, one of the purposes we all have is to help each other unlock the armor we all carry. Sitting with patients in detention centers and on the locked psychiatric inpatient units, listening as they explained atrocities they either experienced or committed against another, I've contemplated often that no doubt the soul had to be locked up tight, particularly for those who experienced marginalization and trauma. For so many, because of the inheritance of our ancestors' stories, our own trauma, experiences, and unprocessed feelings, the world isn't a safe place and the people in it can't be trusted—so the soul has never seen the light of day. And, you've likely guessed by now, the keys to letting walls down often are in finding the safe harbor of a relationship, where you can acknowledge and name those emotions so the soul might be convinced it's safe enough to show itself.

So much of the debate has been whether, at the core, we as humans are good or evil. And I think the answer is both, depending on your history and the situation in which you find yourself. Inherently, however, the good happened first. As Thomas Aquinas wrote, "Good can exist without evil, whereas evil cannot exist without good."

EMOTIONAL INTELLIGENCE

If we're going to talk about the foundation of the healthiest, most connected humans on the planet, it turns out that emotional regulation is but one skill of a larger concept called emotional intelligence (EI).[8] Basically, EI refers to the ability to perceive, control, and evaluate emotions, both in yourself and in others. Emotional intelligence is generally said to include a few skills: emotional awareness, or the ability to identify and name one's own emotions; the ability to harness those emotions and apply them to tasks like thinking and problem solving; and the ability to manage emotions, which includes both regulating one's own emotions when necessary and helping others to do the same. This last component of emotional regulation is the one I think is the big kicker (as we talked about in the first chapter). Overall, I often think about EI as someone's "bedside manner" or how someone is able to "read a room." A person can be remarkably cognitively bright but have no clue how to navigate the emotions necessary in relationships. There are lots of thoughts about the robustness of the concept of emotional intelligence, largely because emotions are harder to measure than cognitive ability. Researchers have, however, largely demonstrated that people with high emotional intelligence have greater mental health, job performance, and leadership skills.[9]

There are an estimated 3,000 English-language words available for describing our emotions. Even with all those options, most of us would still experience feelings for which there are, apparently, no words. Conversely, it's reported that there are an estimated 10,000 Spanish words for five discrete emotions: happiness, disgust, anger, fear, and sadness.[10] So many cultures, in fact, have many more words for emotions than Anglo-Saxon cultures do.[11] Work from a variety of fields—psychology, neuroscience, linguistics, and anthropology—has provided evidence that the way people express and experience emotions may be greatly influenced by our cultural upbringing;[12] however, some big commonalities exist. For example, around the world, our emotional vocabularies seem to be organized in terms of four basic dimensions: words can vary depending on whether the emotions are more or less positive or negative (like love and hate, respectively), active or inactive (like joy and sadness), strong or weak (like rage and dislike), and expected or unexpected (like contentment and surprise).[13]

What happens to you when we start to talk about the "good" emotions—the ones that are the most acceptable, the ones we desire to feel in ourselves and the people we love? I'm guessing that words like "happy," "content," "love," and maybe even "joy" come to mind. We often don't wish ourselves or others to feel the "bad" ones, like sadness, disgust, shame, or fear—when we are regulated, at least. Those "bad" emotions, by nature of how we have defined them socially, means we obviously don't want them.

There's beautiful research around toxic positivity that incites us to just stay positive and "don't be so angry." Some, like psychologist Susan David,[14] have considered our current climate as a "tyranny of positivity." So, we end up in this place of rigid denial that we even have some of those "bad" emotions, further perpetuating the belief that they don't exist, we don't want them, shouldn't acknowledge them, and certainly don't like to see them in others.

NO BAD PARTS?

It's been fascinating to watch people acknowledge all those "parts." The most remarkable shifts, I can confidently tell you, happen when, instead of hiding from them, running from them, or even telling them to fuck off, someone has the courage to just see them—to simply acknowledge them—and, if possible, without judgment. It's magic, really. Every time. In fact, there's ample evidence to support the notion that all the parts are necessary. One of the best at describing this is a guy named Richard Schwartz, a psychologist and author.[15] Schwartz talks about considering ourselves as having many parts that often exist separately, and we're often encouraged to pay mind only to the "good parts." We're taught to believe we have "one mind" out of which different thoughts, emotions, impulses, and urges grow. From this mono-mind point of view, our natural condition is a unitary mind. Unless, of course, some experience, particularly trauma, comes along and shatters it into pieces, like shards of a broken vase.

The mono-mind paradigm has caused us to push away the parts we fear the most, the parts that don't fit or are "bad." And in our attempts to control what we consider to be disturbing thoughts and emotions, we just end up fighting, ignoring, disciplining, hiding, numbing, or feeling ashamed of those parts of ourselves. And then we shame ourselves for not being able to control them when they inadvertently play into our understanding of the world. Schwartz's concept of legacy burdens feels particularly relevant to mention here. Similar to Indigenous teachings around blood memories,[16] and Galit Atlas's concept of emotional inheritance,[17] Schwartz explains that some of us come into this world already wired by the stories of our ancestors. We have essentially absorbed their stories in our beings and carry their burdens. Many have suggested that sometimes these experiences can be even more powerful than our own.[18]

Because of our histories and our own trauma, we build walls around the soul as defenses. For whatever reason (and there are often many for each of us), it wasn't safe to have our tender soul readily available to those around us. We were taught or wired to believe that you don't let people in; they'll hurt you, so be wary, untrusting, and make 'em earn it. Those defenses become the armor for the most vulnerable, confident, engaged parts of ourselves. Those defenses all act as protectors in some ways, and some serve us well in certain moments and then don't in others or become nuisances as we grow and change and no longer need them.

What interests me the most about "bad" emotions is that when we push them aside, they fester, and we start to believe that is our truth. They become amplified. See, our internal pain always needs a place to go. And depending on the amount of safe space available (or lack of it), some of us can go through most of our lives just holding on to that pain. Until we no longer can. And then it starts to eat us, sometimes from the inside out. It starts to show up as neuropsychological, emotional, or physical illness. As I'm writing these words, I keep thinking about the story of my friend Jesse Thistle. A kid who grew up in and out of foster care, homeless, addicted, and incarcerated, he beautifully describes in his memoir, *From the Ashes*,[19] the number of significant, often brief, experiences with other humans that allowed him slowly but surely to believe he was not all of the shame and hate he believed for so long that he was. The time someone asked his name as he sat homeless on a street, or when a shopkeeper he once stole from gave him a hot meal—that's when the armored walls began to subside. He now bravely bares his soul as a beacon to others. Married to a beautiful woman who believed in him before many others did, Jesse is a father, an author, and a university professor. I've sat with him in interviews, and his legacy burdens are palpable. They don't disappear when they are exposed to the world, but there is a freedom that comes in allowing others to bear witness—once someone or something has made it safe to hold space for the potential that is in all of us. See, we were never meant to do any of this alone.

What if we started to consider this discomfort as all just a part of the price of admission? What if we took on this radical acceptance of emotions? Made it clear that accuracy matters when we are trying to identify those feelings we've been trying to fight. What do those feelings mean? What if we invite them to stay, to teach us? What if we ask them why they are there? Now let me be honest: I appreciate right out of the gate that this can happen only in doses that we can handle. I completely understand that we can't be sitting there all the time just bringing on the shit-show of shame and trauma. We're not that good, nor is it necessary. There is a readiness that has to happen before we just dive in—and it often depends on whether there is a regulated other available to help us navigate the rawness of pain. I'm starting to realize that emotions are not random; they are data. They tell us something and, when we don't listen, they turn it up louder and louder and louder until we pay attention. What if we consider that you own your emotions, they don't own you? And it might just be time to create some space to listen to all of them, on your terms.

SO MUCH MORE THAN HAPPY

There seems to be consensus across this planet that the "good" emotions—related to the way many of us feel when we hear the word "happy"—often seem to be the preferred states, not only for ourselves but most especially for the people we love. Sometimes, even at the expense of their own well-being. For those we truly love, we would often sacrifice so much and protect them at almost any cost.

This desire for happiness seems to be most heavily wished upon our children. Indeed, I have said many times: "The only thing I ever want for my kids is for them just to be happy." Conversely, the opposite of this happiness goal is often the reason we sever relationships: "I'm just not happy anymore"; or, "My job brings me no happiness." As divorce rates rise and workplace burnout abounds, I often wonder: Is anybody really happy? And what does it mean to be happy? Should we be expanding our vocabulary around this thing called happiness?

In fact, we want to know about this happy thing so badly that the scientific study of happiness has exploded over the past three decades. Nobel Prize winners Daniel Kahneman and Angus Deaton[20] are leading researchers, as is renowned psychologist Martin Seligman.[21] One of the most prominent in this happiness space of experts is researcher Shawn Achor,[22] who says there is a "happiness advantage" to those who see the world from the perspective of happy. In fact, he calls it the competitive edge experienced by those who are happy and optimistic. Positive emotions make us more productive, healthier, more creative, and better able to process information.[23] From children performing better on tasks, to doctors making better—and quicker—diagnoses, to lower absenteeism in the workplace, Achor asserts that those of us who are happy simply do better.[24] I love his words: "The most successful people, the ones with a competitive edge, don't look to happiness as some distant reward for the achievements, nor grind through their days on neutral or negative; they are the ones who capitalize on the positive and reap the rewards at every turn."

It appears that this mind shift from thinking about all the things that could go wrong to thinking about all the things that could go right is critical. I'm always so interested, however, in the process that underlies this shift and the nagging belief that, regardless of how much time you get to spend in the positive space, the other side of emotion is often equally important and maybe even more so. What we know to be true is that it's not necessarily just being happy that makes us most fulfilled. What if it has much more to do with feeling all of the emotions? What about things like shame, which is what happens in your body when I ask you about regret? Just notice. What about when we say words like "betrayed"? Or "failure"? Or "emptiness"? I think there is so much to this process of emotion that you and I stay numb to our whole lives. Often, we have learned to simply bury our emotions. The collection of emotions remains underneath, but eventually they tend to spill over. In fact, the clinical use of psychedelic drugs has provided a renewed sense of purpose, particularly for those who have experienced trauma, and I think this result has much to do with the giving of permission, in a guided way, to safely feel the things we've so often avoided.

GRIEF—THE OTHER SIDE OF THE SPECTRUM

And what happens when we dive into the deepest ends on the other side of the spectrum? We rarely use words that capture the despair that is grief, like "anguish" and "hopelessness"—words that often swirl around this emotion. Like if I asked you, "What does it feel like in your body to be deeply sad?" Or, "Where do you feel it when you think about your biggest loss?" For a moment, sink into the range of your experience with sadness, from just blue to the unbelievable depths of agony. It seems grief is one of the big emotions that no one wants to talk about;[25] but every single soul you know or love or live with is navigating it, to some degree, this very moment. We like it best when the people we love are calm and connected, and grief is often the opposite of those things. It can be the most disconcerting, debilitating emotion and can feel like physical pain in dark moments. I've had many teachers who have shown me that grief, just like any other big emotion, is best served full on. By pulling up a chair and inviting it to the table. So, since we're here, let's do that together.

Upon reading grief counselor Alan Wolfelt's work,[26] I learned a few things about grief that made this concept more plausible. Wolfelt explained that although these labels are often used interchangeably or together, grief and mourning are two very different things. Grief, by definition, is a natural response to loss. It's the emotional suffering you feel when something or someone you love is taken away. Often, the pain of loss can feel overwhelming. You may experience all kinds of difficult and unexpected emotions, from shock or anger to disbelief, guilt, and profound sadness, to bursting into laughter at the absurdity of it all. Grief (although expressed in a wild spectrum of ways across different genders) is a remarkably universal experience.[27] It tends to be done in isolation, it's unpredictable, and it's often an asshole. Just when you think you're "fine," or it's been years since the loss of someone important to you, suddenly you hear the song, or smell the pierogies—and it drops you to your knees. You pull over to the side of the road to wipe a relentless stream of tears. I, quite honestly, still can't believe this is a universally felt emotion, because it can be so excruciatingly debilitating. Mostly because I think it's so hard to describe. There's no script for how grief is to be experienced, but the one thing I know for sure is that if you have loved and lost, you've experienced grief.

On the other hand, mourning is how you heal. Mourning is defined as how you express grief outside yourself—it's the expression of an experience that is the consequence of loss. Essentially, it's what you do with all the bullshit emotions that make up grief. Unlike with grief, we're not born with the capacity to mourn. You need to be shown how to do it. And again, although mourning is not an emotion, the many emotions that often accompany grief (including joy) need to be demonstrated to process grief. Mourning is often done in relationship with other people because we tend to make sense of the hard things together. Further, so many have explained what Parker Palmer beautifully captured, particularly for those of us in a state of grief: "The human soul doesn't want to be advised or fixed or saved. It simply wants to be witnessed—to be seen, heard and companioned exactly as it is."[28] Although it's difficult to witness, you can't fix grief. But it's so helpful if you have someone who can sit with you in it.[29;30] That's where the mourning—the healing—happens.

In David Kessler's expansion of Elisabeth Kübler-Ross's original five stages of grief model, he suggests that, in fact, there is a sixth stage of grief that is often most necessary for the (eventual) healing process. That sixth stage he's called meaning.[31] I love this so much. Kessler argues that it's finding meaning beyond the stages of grief most of us are familiar with—denial, anger, bargaining, depression, and acceptance—that can transform grief into a more peaceful and hopeful experience. Kessler was the protégé of Kübler-Ross, the original theorist who created the stages of grief.[32] Kessler knew suddenly and painfully how necessary and powerful making meaning of it all became following the sudden death of his 21-year-old son. So beautifully, he writes that "meaning comes through finding a way to sustain your love for the person after their death while you're moving forward with your life. Loss is simply what happens to you in life. Meaning is what *you* make happen."[33]

What constitutes meaning is different for everyone. Kessler makes clear that the meaning is not to be found in the death itself—in the tragedy or by looking on the bright side of a loss. This is impossible, and not conducive to healing. Instead, he and many others have suggested that some people, tormented by a traumatic or unfair death, devote their lives to a relevant cause. This is what mourning looks like: starting a charity, volunteering, or spreading the word about the death to help prevent future tragedies can become what legacies are made of. Others may find purpose in activities and relationships outside the death. Finding meaning means engaging with the world and feeling you have a meaningful place in the community. Tapping into gratitude (a whole section on that coming up), despite the loss, also plays a role in finding meaning.[34]

The disconnection that has happened around the grief and mourning process over the past couple of generations is quite remarkable, fueled most significantly in recent years as restrictions made it unsafe to mourn in large groups for so many across this globe. Think about what happened when somebody died up the road in our parents' generation. I have many memories and have heard many stories of what took place. You would just go. You wouldn't call before or check to see what you should bring in case of any gluten allergies. You would simply show up on the front doorstep with all the kids and all the gluten. You would come in, drink a lot of coffee, and make sense of the hard things. I remember it being commonplace that the body of the dead guy would even be in the house. Death was a part of life. And if you have any context for a situation like this, imagine where the children were. I will tell you; they were at the feet of their parents. Maybe not delving into deep emotion but playing, running around—and, most importantly, also watching. Because you can't tell people how to mourn. You have to show them. Remember, you're born with the capacity to grieve. But someone must show you how to mourn. When given these opportunities, many kids understand very quickly that food is critical, that sometimes people get drunk to show their emotion, and that even in death, laughter is allowed. And when it comes to our babies, I often get asked how old kids have to be before they can go to a funeral. And I will tell you. Without a doubt, if you're old enough to love, you're old enough to grieve. Bring them, so they can feel it, too.

And for the record, even though I know it's important to just go, it doesn't mean it's easy. I've spent many times wondering when it would be the "right time" for me to call or check in on a friend who had a significant loss. For what it's worth, if you're ever on the fence, just go. Show up with your whole heart and all the gluten (or gluten-free) you have. Even if the timing isn't "just right," you'll feel it, and the gesture won't be lost. You can always leave the lasagna on the front porch with a note. And although it's often in the moments or days following a death when we tend to show up, if we're going to at all, don't forget about the importance of the six-month anniversary or the big holidays. That's when we tend to stop feeling seen the most. Just keep showing up for each other. Turns out, in these moments you probably need it as much as they do.

There was a time when I learned that the distance between us really matters when the loss is sudden. And in those moments of making sense of sudden losses, we won't forget the ones who are brave enough to show up. And at some point, we will more likely than not be on the receiving end of needing that grace. One of the scariest honors of my life was being the one to deliver the news.

FEELING ANGUISH

Many can attest to—and probably even more fear—what anguish truly looks like. In my imagination and in my experience, anguish is getting unexpected, life-altering news that would involve the untimely death of someone you love. And we often don't think about the tellers when we think about that experience. Anguish is most often depicted in the person who receives that information.

One unforgettable day, I was on the telling end. When I think about witnessing the receiver's anguish, it pushed new boundaries for me in terms of how far the spectrum of emotion can go. Our story started as roommates. Adiam was from a tiny country called Eritrea and she taught me so much about so many things. She spoke often of her family, and I marveled at how this young, strong woman was forging her new life in a country where she barely knew the language. She was so far from the people she loved. I knew she had siblings she adored who had chosen to stay in their home country to support their parents. I sometimes overheard a phone call from home, and I got to witness the joy as she spoke in the language that was theirs and reconnected to the ones who knew her soul.

After Aaron and I got married, she moved out and got an apartment just a few blocks up the road. Shortly after she moved, I received one of those calls. In broken English, the caller, desperate for me to understand, was asking about Adiam. I tried to explain that Adiam no longer lived with us. The caller slowly explained that they understood Adiam had moved, but they had news they didn't want to deliver to her over the phone. I held my breath as, through tears, the caller explained that Adiam's brother, a couple of years younger than her and with a bright future in law, had been killed in a car accident the night before. The family was devastated, and everyone knew except Adiam. They wanted somebody to be with her when she heard the news and wondered if I could do that for them.

Now, let me take you into what happened in my head over the next minutes. I knew we didn't have time because her family feared news would travel fast and they didn't want her to be alone. I looked at Aaron and said, "I don't know if I can do this"; or, maybe more accurately, "I don't want to be the one to do this." We were pregnant with our first child, and I felt selfishly as though this might be too much. Even as I write these words, I think how ludicrous that sounds, but it's always interesting to me what goes through your head in those few seconds during the gut punch of the hard things. Is there any way to get around it or avoid it? I called Adiam's pastor next. I didn't want to do this by myself.

Thankfully, the pastor's wife agreed to meet me at Adiam's apartment in the next few minutes. It's interesting what can happen in a moment when two strangers realize they have a very important emotion to deliver. After a hug in the parking lot with this woman I'd never met, together we stood silent as we rode the elevator up, looking briefly at each other. I knocked on Adiam's door. She was expecting us, since I had called to say I was wondering if I could drop by. It was 7 AM. She opened the door suspiciously, and she knew. She said, "Hello" and then, "Just tell me who." I said, "Sweetheart, you're right. I am here to tell you some news, and I wanted to bring somebody very important with me." I remember being shocked at the tone in her voice—I'd never heard her yell, let alone scream, as she hurled these words at me: "Just tell me who." And I said, "Your brother, Helmi, was killed last night in a car accident. He died at the scene. Your mom is waiting for your call." And as she fell to the floor and I did, too, all I could think was, *This is a whole new depth of pain that I have never experienced.* Until writing these words, with tears falling on the keyboard, I didn't even realize that was what anguish feels like.

This phenomenal human navigated her anguish valiantly. She let herself feel it. In the days and weeks that followed, we spent a lot of time together, eating, crying, laughing, and trying to figure out how we could get her home. I often think of her, and them, and how difficult the disconnect can be when grief hits—especially when your people are a million miles away. How truly we are wired to be together. How do people navigate war? Or prison sentences? Or deployment? The familiarity of simply looking into the face of another where a history lives can calm an entire system—most often without words. But in just this past generation, particularly in the months when COVID pushed us around the most and wars erupted, the mourning process was often interrupted. Cancelations of funerals, wakes, and celebrations of life, with hopes to do it "later," often were the result. I think we will pay the price for those missed opportunities for many years to come.

BRINGING IT BACK HOME

This spectrum of emotions, wherever we land at any given moment, always plays out in our relationships. Researchers have long tried to understand emotions from a theoretical perspective; however, given the ubiquitous nature of these slippery little suckers, they're hard to measure. It's thus made it so much easier to try and make sense of emotions in measurable ways—like behaviors. Turns out, as we've read so far, we're much more complex than that. We like to feel the good ones and stuff the bad ones. And we really like it when those around us are happy, especially if we love them. The trick is, I think, to understand that all our emotions are just that—emotions. They won't kill you and they're not "bad"— the complications begin when we don't have a place to feel them, make sense of them, and challenge the stories they sometimes tell about who we once were.

As you think about this heavy chapter, consider with me, as we get grounded here, a few things:

1. Notice what happens in your body when you try on words like "glee" or "giddy." Then consider words like "gloom" or "melancholy." Notice where they take you in time and space. Emotions are powerful.

2. Where do you find it easiest to express your emotions— in music, through writing, over coffee? The truth is, there's no right place to put them. Considering your options is sometimes the most important place to start.

3. One of the coolest things about any language you speak is that there are words to describe some things, and sometimes there are words that just don't quite cut it. I've just discovered that you're allowed to make up your own words, too, if there's not one out there that fits. Some of my current favorites: "shitfucked" (a situation that was so bad and just got even badder) and Glennon Doyle's[35] "brutiful" (something that is brutal and beautiful all at the same time). Whatever it takes to name it, jump all in.

CHAPTER THREE

That Relationship Thing

WHERE EMOTIONS COLLIDE

Relationships are, indeed, the place where emotions collide. And it makes sense that those of us who are clearest about how our emotions have developed and how we use our emotions to respond tend to have the healthiest relationships. There are intricacies of connected human interaction that can fall into many conglomerations, like family relationships, romantic relationships, friendships, acquaintanceships, and one-offs that are powerful enough to change your life or fleeting and forgotten. Then, of course, all sorts of nuanced interactions land in and among the dance of it all.

Our relationships rely on our social bonds, and you would think that those of us with the deepest bonds are the healthiest, even if they're with a select few. In one of my favorite books, *The Village Effect*,[1] Susan Pinker (a fellow Canadian psychologist) discovered that in Sardinia, a remote, mountainous Italian island, people live longer than anywhere else in the world, including neighbors on the mainland just 200 miles away.[2] The most significant predictor of the longevity of these people was not that they had better access to food, water, or air quality. It was simply that villagers' lives constantly intersect. They live closer together; they require connection daily to get their groceries and their water. In fact, clean air, being fat, or whether you drink alcohol was not nearly as predictable for healthy longevity as the most powerful predictor: social interaction. And whether the bond is strong or weak, it doesn't matter. Essentially, those who spend more time seeing people around them, regardless of whether they are deeply connected to them or not, are the healthiest among us.

WIRED FOR THEM

Let's say it again here: We are wired for connection. Biologically, if we, particularly infants, disconnect from each other, we die. For longevity purposes, the more social interactions we have, the healthier we appear to be. But what about those people we interact with the most often? Healthy relationships typically involve very lofty words like "honesty," "trust," "respect," and "open communication"—and they take effort and compromise from both sides. There's rarely an imbalance of power. Partners respect each other's independence, can make their own decisions without fear of retribution or retaliation, and share decisions. That's the highlight summary of many of the leading researchers in the world who have dedicated their lives to figuring out how we manage to make our relationships the strongest. It's cliché almost when we hear what it takes to make it happen. It raises the question, however, of why it's so hard to do this and why, so often, so many of us struggle to maintain many healthy relationships.

Let's talk briefly about a couple of those relationships that tend to dictate how we show up in the world, including the relationship to our parents and our intimate partners. (We will talk more later about colleagues and friendships.) First, we're all somebody's child. That fact remains amazing to me most days. We all, each of us, have a biological mother and father. Regardless of the (often complicated) stories we have with them, whether they're alive or not, and notably, if we have a relationship with them, or not, they're still our biological parents. And, second, I want to review the research briefly on marriage—the sanctimonious relationship that still is lauded in most societies as the goal. Although this has changed somewhat within the last couple of decades, let's talk about what is considered important in the relationships most of us are the most interconnected to.

PARENT-CHILD CONNECTIONS

The relationships you have, or don't have, with your parents (however that is defined for you) and your other primary caregivers will shape the way you see the world. We first navigate the concept of emotional regulation by looking at our primary caregivers to judge safety, security, and how we show up in the world. So often, the look in the eyes of our caregivers indicates far more than words. When these relationships are connected and emotional regulation has been modeled (at least some of the time), we see children who are better able to provide healthy connections to their partners and their (potential future) children, while remaining connected to their parents. One of the most significant contributing factors to maintaining these relationships is, as you might have guessed, the ability to understand how to communicate—which means someone has had to show you how to do it. If no one has, and few corrective experiences are available, you'll struggle to be able to give that away to the next generation or potentially even stay well connected to the ones who raised you. Hence, the fallout from intergenerational trauma, which we will dive into shortly.

Here's the one thing I've long believed to be true: The job of tiny humans is to lose their friggin' minds. The job of big people is simply to walk them home. Without the chaos, you cannot learn how to make sense of the mess. The chaos is not the problem. It's how you respond to it that predicts the health or well-being of kids, regardless of age. That relationship will always remain, as will the power differential. Now, there are, of course, complicating factors when disease and aging take over. Children often become caregivers for their parents. The constructs that we create in the parent-child dynamic suggest, however, that we always hope, wish, sometimes long for a parent to be in charge. When there is that stable force within a family system, it appears, the players do better.[3]

In all the people I've had the privilege to counsel, I have never met a parent who didn't love their child to the absolute best of their ability. And that ability to love, at least in part, came from how they themselves were loved. I've also rarely had an in-depth session with anyone where the relationship to their mother(s) or their father(s) wasn't mentioned. And the fact is, those key relationships, regardless of how they played out, tend to matter significantly in how you show up in the world. It doesn't excuse or condone the treatment of any of us who were loved by parents who had no one to teach them how to parent. It's incredibly unfair at times, as well as an often-debilitating job to try to break a history of intergenerational trauma. Sometimes it's the job of those in the "village" to teach the most corrective experiences—because we are, as it stands today, typically better with other people's children. Why, you ask? It's so much easier to stay regulated (and have access to) my best skills when I have less skin in the game but still care deeply. Less pressure to teach or "get it right" means I stay calmer—and have more to give away. Sometimes the greatest gift we provide is becoming the village for the people we love, especially when the resources are thin.

I often say this—when I am regulated and connected: I am an amazing mom (if I do say so myself). In fact, I even wrote a bestselling book called *Kids These Days*,[4] telling you all about how to do it. On my dysregulated, losing-my-friggin'-mind days, however, if you saw me with my own kids, you wouldn't buy the book. Skill is rarely the biggest issue we face as parents. It's having access to it that is the key.

The other thing about parent-kid relationships that I think worth mentioning is the importance of true, connected time. These days, it's so much more about quality than it is about quantity, and I've never been clearer about that. Particularly since so many families navigate part-time connections to their children because of divorce or job commitments, what remains important are the looking and seeing moments. Staying home all day with your children while you are overwhelmed, disconnected, or wishing you were somewhere else doesn't serve them—or you—well. Conversely, assuming you have less influence or connection because you see your children only "on weekends" or during the odd hours of balancing shiftwork is simply not true. When we tell ourselves we're not enough, we are much more inclined to look away. Those of us as parents who inevitably feel "less than enough"—particularly when we are navigating messy divorces or the pull of our careers—are much more likely to jump in with our whole hearts if we are reminded, just a little more often, that we are "more than enough." On my most difficult days, the reminder that I'm doing so many things right, or the reassurance that kids are supposed to talk back and melt down, is the fuel I need to stay in the game. Once again, we were never meant to do any of this alone—especially not be solely responsible for the development of another.

It reminds me of these words by poet and philosopher Kahlil Gibran:

. . . Your children are not your children.
They are sons and daughters of Life's longing for itself.
They come through you but not from you,
And though they are with you yet they belong not to you.

You may give them your love but not your thoughts,
For they have their own thoughts.
You may house their bodies but not their souls,
For their souls dwell in the house of tomorrow, which you can-
not visit, not even in your dreams.
You may strive to be like them, but seek not to make them like you.
For life goes not backward nor tarries with yesterday.
You are the bows from which your children as living arrows are
sent forth.
The archer sees the mark upon the path of the infinite, and He
bends you with His might that His arrows may go swift and
far.
Let your bending in the archer's hand be for gladness;
For even as He loves the arrow that flies, so He loves also the
bow that is stable.[5]

HOLY MATRIMONY

The other big player in the realm of relationships tends to be the status of your intimate ones, however defined. These can involve different combinations—legally recognized or otherwise, including opposite-sex, same-sex, or polyamorous relationships. Typically, these are with the fellow humans you interact with the most and who tend to have the greatest influence on how you show up in your adult world. I've long been interested in just what it takes to make a marriage work. Perhaps that's because I'm the child of divorce. And even though my parents separated from each other for the last time when I was 19 years old, I can tell you that today it remains a significant factor in how I define myself. In my dissertation so many moons ago, I looked at police marriages and what it took to navigate a healthy connection when the injection of frequent and significant amounts of trauma were present.

Matrimony, the state of being married, might be the ultimate dance of giving and taking. And so many of us give it a whirl. Although the numbers of "never-marrieds" have risen in recent years, at any given moment the majority of the world's adult population would identify as "married."[6] When we're in a relationship and acknowledged by another, souls are revealed, if even briefly, and the other typically has (or did have at one point, anyway) the ability to regulate you. That's why we fall in love with another and, understandably, generosity, grace, empathy, and kindness abound. It's a system that psychologist Sue Johnson has so beautifully identified as an infinity loop of connection. I learned most from her model (Emotion Focused Therapy, or EFT) how to navigate couples within the therapeutic process. Essentially, using an attachment lens,[7] Johnson (originally supported by Leslie Greenberg's work),[8] understands that distress in relationships is centered in the loss of secure emotional connection. When this happens, a negative cycle, or "dance," develops as each partner tries to cope with the loss of that connection, usually by defending their soul with responses like anger, criticism, distancing, silence, or relationship distractions. Once established, these negative cycles can crop up over the slightest issue and, over time, are corrosive to the bonds of trust and security in the relationship.[9]

Identifying this "dance" allows couples to have an emotional language to identify when the pattern that starts to push them around arises. One of the more common dance steps is described like this: "When you ask so many questions, I typically shut down.

And when I shut down, you typically try harder to get me to talk. That pisses me off even more, so I talk even less." Understanding a "dance" with your own partner can unlock some of the defenses, allowing for the more vulnerable emotions like understanding, compassion, and empathy to rise. In turn, each partner can then express a more loving, compassionate response.

This whole dance thing in relationships is something you can't unsee once you know it. We all have our patterns. And so often you can't see them when you're in them. I'm not always a fan of knowing my own, but I do like to point them out in others. Just for fun, let's take me for example. I married a smart dude who comes from a fairly traditional family. He admires my intelligence, he claims; however, when neither of us is feeling overly competent, we remind each other that our individual contribution to our marriage is probably the most important. Now, I will tell you the time I most shut down, armor up, or become defensive is the second I think my very own husband is condescending or not honoring my *equal* contribution to this family we're growing. You want to see this girl get fired up? Make me believe you're underestimating me. And guess what happens then? I get argumentative and loud. Guess how my husband reacts? (Insert arm crossing and doubling down.) He will explain more clearly, and usually s-l-o-w-l-y, exactly what I don't understand. Sweet Jesus! Then I'm really mad, and I'm already preparing how I'm going to raise the children alone. I'm telling you, this can go on for a long time or explode in a few quick exchanges. It's not new. When we get into this dynamic and even when I see it, I sometimes don't care and will dig in deeper. Knowing, however, that I can usually break the cycle by first slowing down and understanding gives me more access to empathy. And gives the two of us a better chance. He has that power, too, and when he steps out of the dance first, with an apology or a softer response, I am still amazed, every time, at how quickly empathy can defuse heightened emotion.

Perhaps the two people most synonymous with work in this area of marital research are marital partners and couples therapists John and Julie Gottman.[10] If I were to summarize their work in just a few sentences (of course, 45 years of research is more complex than that), they've taught me that happy couples have a general positive view of each other, built on a foundation of genuine respect for the other. John Gottman says that fondness and admiration are two of the most important elements in a satisfying and long-term relationship. It requires that partners do "small positive things often." Critically connected within these constraints is the ability to communicate with each other. And it's no surprise that it appears as though couples with some ability to connect on an emotional level, particularly when things are difficult or strained, tend to be more successful.

Lastly, I'll mention the popular book *The 5 Love Languages*[11] that I've been asked about a lot. In it, author and radio talk show host Gary Chapman breaks down his key to understanding how communicating needs effectively can stem from knowing not necessarily what to say, but how to communicate it so it can be heard. Chapman suggests there are five different ways people tend to require connection in their most felt sense of expressing and receiving love, including words of affirmation, quality time, receiving gifts, acts of service, and physical touch. It's likely your primary love language will be connected to how love was expressed in your family of origin. Turns out, although significant differences in the marital experience vary vastly among different cultural practices, the ability to be seen and understood by your partner appears to be one of the most important predictors of relationships that make it.

WHAT'S LOVE GOT TO DO WITH IT?

Love is the one emotion so often discussed, but elusively defined. It's different for so many but lauded by all, it seems. Love is the funnest emotion because it can be the defining feature of every relationship that exists—with your pet, your best friend, a lover, your colleague. Even for material things that you can so desperately "love"—like kids with a stuffy or a college kid with their car. (I remember the familiarity and connection I felt for my first car, Mable, a burgundy '88 Mustang sporting a slightly rusted-out hatchback. That old girl and I drove many miles, and she held many tears. I loved that car.)

When it comes to our children and our intimate life partners, love is apparently the goal. And you can see that when we consider this a worthy definition of love: "We cultivate love when we allow our most vulnerable and powerful selves to be deeply seen and known, and when we honor the spiritual connection that grows from that offering with trust, respect, kindness, and affection." Well—son of a gun—of course that love-drunk feeling is the desire. Who wouldn't want to be in a place where an emotion can unlock that soul—the best part of us!? Even in that definition, I am reminded of the riskiness of the business that is love because embedded in that huge desire for soul-bared freedom comes huge responsibility—the trust and respect part. Because, sweet mother, when you are gifted the entrance to the soul of another via the love emotion, you'd better not fuck it up. Yet so many of us do. All the time (more on that in a bit). Let's just say that it's the mystical, mysterious one of all emotions. And so many creatives among us have attempted to capture it in music and poems and paintings. Expressing its essence seems slightly different for each of us. But it's undeniably understood when you see it—or, maybe better yet, when you feel it.

The kiss of death, if you will, in relationships has, from the Gottmans' perspective, been boiled down to one thing: contempt. In fact, "contempt is fueled by long-simmering negative thoughts about one's partner." John Gottman describes contempt as far beyond criticism, because it indicates a moral superiority over one's partner. And what is so fascinating is that there's a notable change in our physiology when we're in a state of contempt for another. I don't think this contempt thing ever happens overnight. But holy smokes, when we don't talk about the little things, or even have somewhere to put the things that piss us off, they tend to grow. I'm often amazed when we find ourselves willing to not talk about things because we don't want to "rock the boat." If we truly knew that a little boat rocking every now and then would likely ward off a fucking tsunami in a couple years, we'd be far more open to the rocking. I truly don't think it's because any of us wants the tsunami to come. It's just that so many of us have never driven a boat before, and we don't have the first clue what to do when we see the storm clouds coming. Basically, we just keep driving and hope the storm passes. (How's that for an analogy?) Alas, if fondness for each other is completely missing and contempt for the other has largely set in, the marriage won't be a place of sanctity for either party.

In an attempt to simplify the explanation of their research, the Gottmans invite us to consider those couples struggling in a relationship as "the disasters," with those figuring it out as "the masters." They explained that the disasters showed all the signs of arousal—of being in fight-or-flight mode—in their relationships. A conversation between spouses sitting next to each other was like facing off with a huge threat. Even when they were talking about pleasant or mundane facets of their relationship, they were prepared to attack and be attacked. This sent their heart rates soaring and made them more aggressive toward each other. For example, each member of a couple could be talking about how the day had gone, and the highly aroused partner might say to the other, "Why don't you start talking about your day? It won't take you very long."

The masters, by contrast, showed low physiological arousal. They felt calm and connected, which translated into more experiences of warm and affectionate behavior, even when they fought. It's not that the masters had, by default, a better physiological makeup than the disasters. But the masters had created a climate of trust and intimacy that made both more emotionally and thus physically comfortable. I'm fascinated by how, based on our own stories, we can show up for the people in our lives. (And we undoubtedly all come with "legacy burdens" that contribute to our understanding of how relationships work.) So—just to bring it all back to the boat analogy—it's a thing you gotta practice. Those "masters" didn't arrive as skippers. They weathered a few of the storms by taking them head on or dropping the anchor and just waiting it out. I think it has something to do with addressing the situation and, mostly, about renegotiating efforts for when (not if) the next storm comes.

That leads me to this concept of repair—maybe the most important skill that each of us can take into our love lives or our team meetings or our boardrooms. This reconnecting and looking to see again after the storm is one of the most significant skills we will ever learn.

REPAIRING AFTER COLLISIONS

As we wrap up this chapter, ending it on a note about repair feels right. Yet another rockstar psychologist, Harriet Lerner, has so masterfully pointed out in her book (which I've read to Aaron), *Why Won't You Apologize? Healing Big Betrayals and Everyday Hurts*,[12] having the ability to repair when, not if, things go "off the rails" can be the most important saving grace in any important relationship, especially our intimate ones. There are a couple of critical facts about apologies I've learned over the years that I'm going to tuck in right here, just in case you might need them.

First, for an apology to be effective, it can't include the word "but"; otherwise, it erases the apology.[13] Let me tell you, apologizing without a "but" is sometimes nearly impossible. I think about how difficult it is sometimes to apologize to our (read: "my") partner: "Honey, I'm sorry I was yelling at you this morning. I was exhausted . . ." (See, right here, in the space that follows this statement, if you've ever been in this position, I promise you will feel the word "but" rising into your larynx. It might be nearly impossible not to have these words shoot out of your lips: ". . . but if you would just not leave your shit everywhere and help the kids make their lunches once in a while, I might not have to lose my friggin' mind.") Here's the deal: An apology is all about stating what you're sorry for and not prefacing it. Ever. Especially with a "teachable moment" just thrown in at the end because it looks like they're finally listening. A "but" erases the apology. Every time.

And second, an apology also doesn't sound like this: "I'm sorry you're so sensitive." Or, "Sorry, I didn't know this was going to be such a big deal." That's where condescending tones take over and it's so easy to jump into the realm of shame. Half-hearted apologies, where we're looking to unload some of the burden, are rarely received well. Expressing regret, accepting responsibility, and making amends is identified as critical in this process.[14] However, given the unthinkable experiences we sometimes find ourselves in with our partners, actions most always speak louder than words.

There are a million configurations of relationships, and we will continue to talk about some of those as we journey through these pages together. But in the healthiest relationships most common to us all, what appears to be important is an understanding of your (and their) emotions. What's most important, perhaps, is to have some ability to feel empathy for the other person when, not if, the dance of relationship gets interrupted, tested, soured, or scorned. The ability to stay connected, to repair and work through bruised and battered emotions, seems to be critical in this dance of relationships, whether we stay connected forever or not.

WHEN TO ABORT MISSION

As we've discussed, many marriages and long-term relationships end either in separation or divorce. Are there times in relationships when this is not only necessary, but also safest and in the best interests of the entire family system? The answer is absolutely yes. If one party or both parties are unable or unwilling to alter the pattern of contempt that has developed (for whatever reason), the repeated soul-crushing exchanges are not healthy to experience or witness. The destructive patterns that marred the marriage, however, often continue to exist even after divorce. The truth is, I've never seen anyone go through an "easy" divorce, particularly when children are involved. We will dive more deeply into the ending of relationships as we navigate the next chapter, on trauma.

BRINGING IT BACK HOME

Relationships. How can this entity that we need so desperately also be the place where the most pain lives? The complexity of it all exhausts me some days and, at the next turn, gives me so much hope and solace. In our most common relationships—with our primary caregivers (however you define that) and within the relationships we intimately step into—so much unfolds. How we've been loved so often determines, at least to some degree, how we are able to provide love. It doesn't mean we can't learn and unlearn. In fact, that's the sole reason I love what I do so much: We grow better and (hopefully) more connected if we do the work, in each generation that passes, and if we understand how our experiences shape us. Maybe most importantly, if we are given the opportunities or have the experience to truly be seen by others, we are better equipped to give that away.

So far, we've set the stage by knowing that although we're wired for connection, we are in a state of increasing disconnect, fueled by a lack of an emotional language, which makes repairing more difficult. I think it's time to truly consider what the cost of disconnection looks like these days. It's so critically, if not painfully, important to know what we're dealing with if we ever hope to remedy it. Before we do, I want you to consider a few things in this realm of relationships:

1. Consider the relationships you have learned the most from—either the ones you were involved in or the ones you witnessed. What are some of the beliefs you have about how relationships work (or don't work) based on these experiences?

2. Have you ever identified typical patterns of connection and pulling away in any of your close relationships? What role do you typically play? Does this change in your different close relationships or does your role stay fairly consistent?

3. What are your experiences with apology and repair? Think about the times you (if ever) received or gave a genuine apology and consider what it felt like.

CHAPTER FOUR

Trauma
THE DESTRUCTION OF EMOTIONAL SAFETY

Deep breath, and drop those shoulders. Sometimes even the word "trauma," for so many of us, gets our bodies prepared to fight. Know it's okay to walk through this chapter slowly, because trauma, I think, is one of the most important experiences to consider as we navigate the necessary steps in the dance of modern relationships. In fact, if I dare be so bold, I think trauma is one of the biggest reasons we struggle to truly see one another these days. I think we have all experienced it to a certain degree, and I think the more we have of it in our histories and in our current relationships, the more difficult it becomes to truly see and be seen.

Trauma, from my clinical experience, can be most easily defined as any experience encoded in terror. Why, you ask, would experiencing something while in a state of terror be one of the greatest threats to our emotional well-being and subsequently debilitate us in our efforts to have healthy relationships? See, when you encode something in terror, for the physical protection of your body, your lid flips. You don't need access to the information in your prefrontal cortex, so your brain does this very primitive, helpful thing and it flips all your ability to make sense of it, or truly feel it, right out of the way. This helpful skill, especially when you're really going to die or are in significant danger, gives you easier access to your limbic system, where those most primitive and protective emotional regulation skills to keep you alive—fight, flight, and freeze—can be accessed.[1]

After the threat has passed, however, there is a necessary step of making sense of that experience once you have returned to safety, calmed the body, and your prefrontal cortex has come back on. The process gets messed up when there's nowhere to come down to from the traumatic experience and reintegrate the emotions. And you can well imagine, if you stack a few of these difficult experiences on top of one another (or years and years of these experiences on top of one another), just what the ramifications might entail. Sometimes, children live in this heightened state of arousal for many of their waking hours; families have lived generations largely in this state; or people work entire careers without having much opportunity to integrate these intense emotional experiences. One of my favorite insights, so eloquently explained by psychiatrist Bessel van der Kolk, goes like this: "Managing your terror all by yourself gives rise to another set of problems—dissociation, despair, addictions, a chronic sense of panic, and relationships that are marked by alienation, disconnections, and explosions."[2] Whew! That's a heavy string of words, which carries with it the significant role this thing called trauma—and the isolation that's often associated with many people's experiences with trauma—plays in the most disconnected parts of our world.

In fact, many traumatic experiences in relationships, including things like abuse, infidelity, and divorce, involve betrayal by another person.[3] Workplace burnout has also been identified as a significant price to pay that I think deserves its own chapter (stay tuned). Although these are not particularly light considerations, I would say it's a combination of abuse, betrayal, and workplace stress that presents most frequently in my office. Just a reminder: Even as I write these words, I'm assuming you will be thinking, "I thought this was going to be an uplifting read." But stick with me. Because we can no longer Mary Poppins the fuck out of this "we're fine, I'm fine" bullshit. We can't address what we don't first acknowledge. And I've never yet met a single soul who hasn't gone through a little hell. Yes, some of us have way more difficult stories than others. But the notion of comparative suffering—where we think that others might have it worse than us or that our story doesn't deserve to be told—often keeps us from identifying our own story; or, conversely, believing we can rise if we're on the worst end of it all.[4] We must hold space for the hard stuff first, however that looks for us.

PRESENT-DAY DISCONNECT

You'll recall from our earlier chapters that people who are most emotionally dysregulated are often experiencing uncertainty, fear, and the sense that there's no end in sight (no clear plan). With that in mind, consider the components of a global pandemic. Uncertainty, fear, and no end in sight. Understandably, if we've lived in a heightened state of arousal for years as a planet, there has to be a cost. Indeed, the statistical evidence is starting to compile. The *National Law Review* has reported that particularly in the wake of the global pandemic, divorce rates have increased by 34 percent across the United States, Asia, and the United Kingdom, with early indications that Canada is following suit.[5] Intimate partner violence has risen for the fifth year in a row and child maltreatment numbers are the highest we've seen them in this lifetime.[6] Systemic oppression and racial disparity in our classrooms and in our communities are very much present, and only in very recent years have we begun discussing this situation more readily.[7] And even before the COVID 19 pandemic, depression was the leading cause of debilitation in young adults. When you add stress to any system or object, if there were cracks in the foundation before, they now become most apparent. These numbers reflect it. And, in turn, I suspect a mental health crisis is well underway.

There are some specific experiences I want to explore in this section that in no way are exhaustive. However, the experiences of abuse, infidelity, and divorce are factors that have, especially within the context of developing present-day relationships, become increasingly common and need our attention before we can ever hope to approach them differently.

THE INJURIES OF ABUSE

You cannot experience abuse without experiencing trauma. The only other experience that is deeply connected with and insepar-able from trauma is racism,[8] and we will talk about that more in the next chapter. Although it can take many forms, abuse falls into four general categories: physical, sexual, and emotional abuse, and neglect.[9] And at the heart of most every abusive exchange is emotional dysregulation. Typically, when we cannot get a need addressed or when we're not heard, coupled with a shortage of emotional regulation skills, we will seek connection in a way that violates the rights and/or safety of another. Typically, abuse hap-pens at the hands of another person—the same being (or beings) who we are supposedly wired for connection to. Abuse becomes particularly debilitating when there was a previous relationship with the abuser that was deemed safe, and this, sadly, is the story for many victims, as most of them generally know their abuser. For example, victims of sexual assault know their attacker in approximately eight of 10 cases. When a child is the victim of sexual abuse, the rates are even higher—90 percent of victims know their attacker. In fact, the most common traumas to women occur at the hands of their intimate partners, and the most common traumas to children occur at the hands of their parents.[10] Child abuse and domestic violence are often inflicted by people who are supposed to love you. In the last couple of years, there was an initial thought that we might have better opportunities to connect to our children because of pandemic restrictions. However, among children 5 years and older, the number of child abuse victims tripled compared to a similar period before the pandemic.[11]

In 2019, the percentage of victims of child maltreatment with caregivers who abused alcohol or other substances increased,[12] even more significantly than before the pandemic, when there was already a strong statistical link between child maltreatment and parental substance abuse. An easily understandable cycle occurs: When you haven't received love, support, and connection, you can't give it away. Further, feelings of exhaustion and being overwhelmed (common parental experiences) arise. Subsequently, you feel awful and numb those emotions the best you can, even if it means temporary escapes—potentially with alcohol or drugs—and, subsequently, have less access to your prefrontal cortex.

Further, and not surprisingly, child neglect and maltreatment are likely to create consequences for victims later in life. In one of the largest research studies examining childhood trauma to date, researchers of the Adverse Childhood Experiences[13] have repeatedly confirmed that there is an undeniable cost to family disconnection. Abused children are 25 percent more likely to experience teen pregnancy, and teens who have experienced abuse are more likely to engage in sexual risk-taking behaviors, putting them at greater risk for sexually transmitted diseases. Further, that pending mental health crisis we talked about is no surprise. And, of course, the financial cost of child abuse and neglect in North America is staggering—estimated at between $124 billion and $585 billion annually in the United States.[14]

When we see rates of child abuse increase, it would be every expectation that we'd also see rates of domestic violence rise. I'm not sure which one of these interactions comes first, but that point is moot. What we know to be true is that when one rate is high because of increased dysregulation and a lack of resources to hold space for it all, typically so is the other. If you come into that relationship unable to express your needs in a healthy or regulated way, "turning it up" to get your needs met may be more likely to occur as the relationship settles in—and you stand more to lose if the other pulls away. Rates of domestic violence (which can include one or all three kinds of abuse) have been rising year over year in Canada for the past decade.[15] More specifically, one in three women and one in four men have experienced some form of physical violence by an intimate partner. This includes a range of behaviors (e.g., slapping, shoving, pushing). In Canada, 44 percent of women reported experiencing in their lifetime some form of psychological, physical, or sexual violence by an intimate partner.[16] Further, violence against women tends to increase in any emergency, including epidemics.[17] Stress, disruption of social and protective networks, increased economic hardship, and decreased access to services can exacerbate the risk of women suffering violence.

Outside of the home, the public continues to be inundated with news of multiple cases of abuse within institutions such as the Canadian military[18] and the Indian residential school system,[19] and in sports organizations including the United States gymnastics team,[20] the National Hockey League,[21] and junior hockey organizations.[22] It astounds me that so much reporting of abuse remains shrouded in secrecy, particularly when men report abuse, and is covered up because of a fear of social ruin. And while we're just beginning to talk about so many atrocities that have happened within our own reach, so much abuse of power and position continues to happen as a reflection of systemic and gender oppressive structures that remain firmly in place in many organizations and cultures.[23]

EMOTIONAL INJURIES ARE PHYSICAL INJURIES

Here's one of the (many) reasons why it's important to keep talking: Trauma can quickly become a physical injury since emotional experiences can so profoundly impact the brain and subsequently become deeply life altering. The prefrontal cortex we were talking about earlier allows us to absorb and integrate the experiences and learnings of thousands of generations who have come before us. When it's in a heightened state of arousal, you're more susceptible to trauma. Unpredictability, overt chaos, threat—those are the things that change the brain.[24;25] When you feel unsafe for long periods of time, the brain starts to change. What it takes to heal (as we will soon talk about in much greater detail) is rhythmic conversation and safe connections. However, by virtue of dysregulation, these experiences of predictability and calm are often inaccessible to people in a heightened state of arousal. Anybody who feels dysregulation needs the regulation of relationship, and we are in a state of poverty in relationships.[26]

So here's the point about the ever-increasing experiences of abuse: The more dysregulated we become, the more difficult it is to lean into each other. And the understandable tendency is, we stop looking and seeing each other, and ultimately we become disconnected. You can appreciate the concern about the ever-decreasing nature of connected relationships; if we're getting less of what we need, future generations are going to have to struggle even more significantly to give it away. And sometimes, even when we are heard (but more especially when we don't feel like we are), there's an overwhelming need for connection that results in our seeking it somewhere outside of our closest partner (or partners). The intricacies involved in infidelity have long been talked about and are a necessary stopping point in this section on trauma, I think, because infidelity rarely ends up being just about two people. The understandable need for connection is present, but the betrayal that is often involved leaves the potential for significant trauma within an entire family system.

THE STATE OF AFFAIRS

According to the American Psychological Association, infidelity is defined as the situation in which one partner in a marriage or other intimate relationship becomes sexually or emotionally involved with a person other than the person's spouse or partner.[27] Also called cheating, it usually transpires in secrecy. In fact, infidelity remains the number one reason that married and common-law relationships end.[28]

When people make a commitment to each other to be faithful, and that commitment gets broken, rarely is the betrayal welcomed. The experience is often "encoded in terror" when one party understands they're no longer a part of a dynamic they thought they were part of. When betrayal becomes confirmed (even in the cases when there is a sense that it might be occurring), the resulting debilitating emotions often include hurt, shame, shock, and humiliation and require a place to safely be discussed. Typically, the very person (or people) who betrayed you used to be the place you might go first. Understandably, the ability to remain open, to appreciate all the sacrifices that you made to get you to a particular destination as a couple, become significantly questionable. For example, I often hear separating couples say, "I gave up my career for you" or "I moved my whole life to this town for you," and "the only reason we had another child was because you wanted it." Once someone's stepped away from the dance, all those things that were once gladly sacrificed for the common good become very much a part of a scorecard.

Historically, affairs were considered to be real only when there was a physical betrayal—when two people "hooked up." This earlier definition made sense because there were few other ways to secretly communicate unless you planned to meet up with another. Now when we think about the convenience of social media and the instant accessibility to each other, there's more and more discussion around what constitutes an emotional affair and how that may or may not affect your marriage. What's wrong with having just somebody to lean into to talk to or get excited about your life? When does it become an affair and not just a friendship?

Just imagine you're having a particularly difficult day, you're feeling like a shitty parent, you're disconnected from your spouse, and you're scrolling Facebook or Instagram. And because you often have mutual connections, people you used to know magically pop up on your feed, even if you don't follow them directly. And there you are, sitting in your jammies at night drinking your tea, the kids are in bed, you're trying to avoid your partner, and you come across a profile of the person you dated in college and just send them a message. It's innocent. It's just you checking in. We're so disconnected in this world, aren't we? We should be engaging in relationships more, right? And then, suddenly, the "Oh my gosh how are you? You look great" starts to happen, and you're on a slippery slope that you honestly never intended to be on. And that is the beginning of a waterfall of connections where there's been so much emptiness. It feels familiar and maybe even justifiable, because of course you had that relationship long ago. You know about their family, or they know about yours. And suddenly, maybe even legitimately so, we start to wonder why we settled for the things we have.

As you can probably tell from how often I reference her work, particularly her book *The State of Affairs*, I love psychologist Esther Perel, whose very nonjudgmental, insightful work purports that if you are stepping out of a marriage there are three things that are probably in place: secrecy, emotional involvement, and sexual alchemy. Let's just unpack those real quick. It stands to reason that any infidelity is organized around secrecy. Open marriages, including polyamorous arrangements, are becoming more popular, where seeing multiple people in a previously-agreed-on understanding means that for some relationships, stepping out of the marriage is not only expected but encouraged. However, when there is the necessity of secrecy, Perel would say we have checked the first box of infidelity. It's important to note that often we do things that our partners are not aware of, and we use thinly veiled excuses like "I don't want to hurt them," "It doesn't mean anything," or "I don't want them to have to worry about it" that can often kick-start a spiral into secrecy.

Next is emotional involvement, a bit trickier to define, but essentially, if you're going to someone else to share parts of yourself with another, this is a strong indicator that connections are splintering. This becomes difficult to define at times because we often engage in office relationships where we rely on our workplace partners, sometimes complicated for those who work in confidential environments. Emotional encounters range from casual, paid, anonymous, and/or virtual sex to deeply involved affairs that claim to enable one to transcend to a new meaning of love and human existence—often including the sense that "I never knew you could feel this way" in a relationship.

Most interesting for me is the concept of sexual alchemy. As Perel explains: "When I asked people all over the world what they experience in infidelity, they said that they feel alive for the first time in a long time. They experience a sense of energy, of renewal, of vitality."[29] So many people I see in my office assume that it was about the sex that someone had with another; the image of that haunts them. But as we've read, it's so much more than the sex—the secrecy and the feeling alive seem to be the things. And these days, it's so much easier to access those feelings of alchemy.

I would completely agree when I think about the growing number of people who have trusted me with their stories of just desperately wanting to be seen by another, even at the risk of hurting those they love. It seems that this experience of alchemy, in particular, clouds their perception of the long-term consequences or potential effects on those involved in the affair, the person or people they'd never otherwise consider hurting. I remember a client long ago explaining that there was never an intention to end up with "so many feelings"; however, now that they were there, so much was worth risking to keep that alchemy alive.

Now, infidelity is not a new phenomenon; there is a sordid history documented across cultures, races, and religions.[30] Researchers from peer-reviewed (i.e., legitimate) studies estimate that 30 to 60 percent of men and 20 to 50 percent of women admit to at least one extra-marital affair in their lifetime.[31] Although it saddens me, the rates of infidelity do not surprise me, nor do I ever think that anyone (including me) is immune to it. When we think about this world as more disconnected now, what has remained is the need for connection. And with our partners, although we spend time together, the question for me becomes more about the quality of that connection. Today, more than ever before, although we're in the same house as the people we love, there are days and even weeks when we never truly have to interact. Further, social media has opened a whole new window of easily accessible, instant opportunities for connecting, perpetuating our lack of any requirement to look at and see the people we live with.[32]

Most interesting to me about affairs is often the root cause. So many times, it has so much more to do with being seen than it does about the act of sexual transgressions.[33] Unless a torrid one-night stand just happens (like in romance novels), there is an emotional connection that takes place first. And here's where the disconnect perpetuates this issue. The idea of safety and security while wanting adventure and novelty collided when we were more connected in our communities. We had the opportunities to be able to have other people provide those things. It is and will always be impossible for one person to be everything for us.

By its very nature, an affair is indeed selfish. And in many instances, understandable, given the context and the necessity for connection. I get how easily it can happen—why people connect or reconnect to other people. I really do. It doesn't mean it doesn't hurt. I just know how much we want to know we matter and when we don't, we get very determined to find some way to feel we do. The desire to see and be seen is remarkably compelling (apparently so much so that I thought we needed a whole book about it). I want to know more about how we get there so often, given the significant fallout of trauma for so many when we betray some relationships for others.

SO, IT'S NOT ABOUT THE SEX?

Glennon Doyle's widely acclaimed memoir *Untamed*[34] opened many conversations about what it means to be caged by internalized misogyny, religious doctrine, and homophobia. It's a brave story of coming out while stepping into oneself. As I have conversations with my own children about their understanding of relationships and gender identity, I am surprised (in a proud way) at the openness many kids I get to meet and work with have when it comes to talking about who they're attracted to and how they identify. Recently, an 11-year-old beautifully explained to her mom that she thinks she is bisexual. And this brilliant mama told me she reeled slightly—silently, internally—but steadied herself with questions and reassurances. This mom responded with, "Tell me more." Her daughter explained, "Why would you limit half the population if you're looking to feel love from somebody else?" Smart girl, that one.

In the numerous relationships I've watched attempt to navigate infidelity, one thing is clear: What many are trying to find is the feeling of being seen. That search is at the core of the connection, which often happens in the innocence of a new relationship, when it's so much easier to access the soul. Why? Often because, between those two souls, there's so much less to lose. What I also notice, however, is that when people end a relationship because of an affair or seek quickly to replace another for the sake of feeling seen, once that spark wears away, the same layers of protective emotion start to take hold and the same issues repeat themselves. The soul becomes harder and harder to access. And here's what's interesting about the innocence of deeply committing to one person, particularly if you have children with them: Although you have a connection with another, the imprint of the person who was allowed closest to your soul will never be filled again. But along with the sexual alchemy with a new partner, we still desperately want familiarity. Truth is, we can't have both. The imprint left behind from one cannot be easily replaced by another. Each (meaningful) relationship that comes and goes in your life had one important thing—connection. And no two individuals will connect with you in the same way. Sometimes, a disconnection is a healthy move to make way for a more engaged connection where two parties come together, having grown from and into ways to access their souls more easily. Divorce can lead to that option, when and if the walls that are there can be addressed or, at the very least, softened slightly.

GOING THROUGH THE BIG D
(AND I DON'T MEAN DALLAS)

Not all infidelity lands us here, in the land of divorce. In fact, some of the most life-changing experiences come out of an affair that spurred long overdue discussions and rebuilding. But often, these days, our lack of an emotional language contributes to our inability to stay connected to the one person who once had access to our soul. It's not surprising, perhaps, that in North America, about 50 percent of married couples divorce,[35] and even more second marriages end in divorce.[36] The most reported contributors to divorce include infidelity, conflict/arguing, and a lack of commitment.

What does that mean? Are we getting worse at this marriage thing? (Yes, I think so.) In the good old days, did couples just have to stay together? (Maybe.) Or did they do better because they had the opportunities to look at each other more often? (Maybe.) I also found this statistic interesting: Having friends who are divorced can greatly increase your chances of becoming divorced yourself.[37] Why might that be, you ask? Once again, we're wired for connection. We want to feel seen and heard. When you're watching a friend go through the throes of pain that divorce brings, you likely feel their pain. However, when they start to date again and re-engage in the divine experience of truly being seen by another, it's often a desired state. You want a piece of that, too.

I think it's interesting in this season of my life, while I sit here writing these paragraphs, that some of the people I love the most have traveled along or are now on this journey of separation and divorce. And I'm not naive enough to fail to consider that I too might be there some day. I am, admittedly, as a child of parents whose marriage didn't make it to the finish line, sensitive to the possibility. And there are countless situations where a divorce is, without a doubt, the healthiest choice for both parties and their families. And there are many other relationships where one of the partners has decided the relationship is over, rendering any efforts at connection pointless. It feels different witnessing separation and divorce through the eyes of a wife and a parent; it's like watching what it means to try to navigate not only the end of a relationship, but the separation of two (or more) families who were so integrated, regardless of whether they got along. And separation from children can be gut-wrenching. This process of separation and divorce is so heavy on the heart. It's about the stories that don't just end with the signing of a paper.

Oftentimes I don't think there is the capacity for lonely, disconnected, and sometimes broken hearts to think about what it might feel like to navigate the future weddings and grandbabies and funerals that will bring people into the same space, even though you're no longer together. This is particularly important if you share children. So, for what it's worth, in this season of big, huge, fat disconnection, what I think is critical when we know that every one in two of us is going to walk this path, is that navigating it alongside each other with as much grace as possible is ultimately best for everyone—namely for you. Even when stories go in different directions, I hope we get better at putting in place the structures that promote empathy. It's going to become so very important in these next few decades. That I know to be true.

BRINGING IT BACK HOME

Although many experiences are generally *always* "encoded in terror," like abuse and even infidelity, many others can be considered traumatic for some and not others, depending on our previous understandings and the resources we had (or didn't have) at the time the experience became a part of our story. What is so critical for me in this season of disconnect is to note a recent increase in instances of traumatic experiences. Coupling that increase with the fact that we seem to have fewer and fewer opportunities to process these emotionally charged experiences while being truly seen and heard, the concern for the mental health crisis that will result honestly keeps me up at night. I worry about the kids who have nowhere to put their big emotions. And I worry about the big people who desperately want to do better, and be better, but have few people who, they think, believe in them. I also know we were never meant to do this alone. And the subsequent lack of connected, safe relationships that appear to become more and more difficult to navigate (in the long term, anyway) makes me wonder about the predictability and stability required for a truly regulated next generation.

And with all of that—deep breath. Drop those shoulders. That was a lot and, no doubt, as you journeyed through this chapter, you thought of all the relationships that mean the most to you. Before we tend to a few more contributors to a disconnected world, contemplate the following:

1. If you're able, consider any experiences that you may have "encoded in terror" and either had or didn't have somewhere to make sense of it all. Just notice how you react to those different experiences today.

2. How easy (or difficult) is it to judge someone you know (even yourself) who has experienced an affair as part of their relationship? Pay close attention to your own story.

3. If you have walked through divorce or know someone who has, reflect on the times when the people involved handled things well; when it appeared that the "new normal" was established and things were regulated. What were the biggest contributors to the events unfolding this way?

CHAPTER FIVE

The Weight of Our Workplaces
FEELING INVISIBLE IN OUR JOBS

S o far, we've discussed relationships as the foundation to feeling seen. Emotional regulation and having an emotional language facilitate this sharing of the soul, while the acts of both abuse and infidelity involve direct experiences with people who have betrayed a relationship. What we often miss, I think, when considering our ability to show up in this world is how our work (either at home or in a formal office space) plays a critical role in both seeing and feeling seen, particularly today as we rely less and less on face-to-face connections with our colleagues. Now that most people (still men more than women) work "outside the home,"[1] the concept of how work comes home is becoming increasingly important. And I can tell you, while sitting in the therapist's chair, the concerns I hear almost as often as the disconnection with partners and kids is probably the stress and struggle of feeling appreciated at work.

CULTURE CLUB

As I write this chapter, I am smack in the throes of building my own company. And getting the workplace culture right seems to be all the rage—and so much easier to create on paper. Although I've worked for a few different institutions in my time, I never considered all that goes into creating policies that govern things like attendance, dress code, code of conduct, hiring, compensation, performance-based pay, inclusive policies and practices, internal transfer, and promotion. Clarity around a mission and a vision—and then writing all that shit down and, even more important, walking the talk—is so much more complex than I imagined. Even as I type those words, I'm overwhelmed and completely unsure of whether we're doing the things I said we would be doing. And although I've heard this from many amazing leaders, no words have ever been truer: It's how you manage the people that is far more important (and far more work) than any product or service you provide. I read these words by Sir Richard Branson early in this journey and they continue to resonate so deeply: "Train people well enough so they can leave. Treat them well enough so they don't want to." I want to work for someone who believes that, and I want to lead like someone who embodies it.

I am in awe of people who have done it well—entrepreneurs who seem to have figured it out; leaders in corporate or government institutions who have navigated the specifics necessary to create places where people can grow. There are a lot of brilliant examples of how to build a successful culture. Writer and entrepreneur James Clear[2] has been a guiding force with these simple words: "You do not rise to the level of your goals. You fall to the level of your systems." It seems there are universal truths in strong teams across industries, and it's no surprise that it comes down to how employees are treated. It turns out, culture and leadership are inextricably linked. It seems that when leaders understand the importance of relationship and connection, while not tolerating bullshit within their employee structure, they perform remarkably better. It seems simple enough in theory. In practice, however, the magnitude of literature in this area seems to indicate that many still struggle to figure it out—or perhaps perpetuate it consistently.

The cost of difficulties at work has played a significant role in the overall well-being of humans. And the buzzword of the decade just may be "burnout," with good reason. The nauseating discussion of work-life balance has seemingly been replaced with "How to just fucking survive till the next holiday." In fact, across many industries, relationships overall have deteriorated significantly in recent years.[3] Essentially, work, regardless of profession, used to be a whole lot funner than it is today, and the costs are becoming too great to ignore. So with that, lets jump into the construct of workplace burnout and why I think organizational cultures will be significant and critical infrastructures to consider if we ever truly want to get reconnected (and assist in the mental health crisis of disconnection) in this modern world.

THE BURNOUT BANDWAGON

The concept of work being something that significantly contributes to the demise of our collective mental health is relatively new. But we've known since at least the 1970s, when more and more people started working outside the home, that there was a cost to not attending to the dynamics that evidently occur. Burnout was a term coined in 1974 by German psychologist Herbert Freudenberger.[4] Almost 50 years ago, Freudenberger was one of the first to describe the consequences of severe stress and "high ideals," particularly at work. Burnout, he said, has three components: First, emotional exhaustion. Second, something he called depersonalization (losing all empathy and compassion).

The third component is a decreased sense of accomplishment (it all feels futile).

Between lost productivity, employee disengagement, absenteeism, lower organizational commitment, and turnover, burnout costs organizations in the United States as much as $190 billion annually.[5] The Mental Health Commission of Canada has similar statistics on workplace mental health. In any given week, 500,000 Canadians don't go to work because of a psychological health issue.[6] Even though over 200 million workdays are lost due to mental health conditions each year, mental health remains a denied reality. In fact, almost 60 percent of employees have never spoken to anyone at work about their mental health status.[7]

DECONSTRUCTING WORKPLACE DESTRUCTION

The original theory that Freudenberger proposed still stands in the most recent research.[8] When the big three—emotional exhaustion, a lack of compassion, and an experience of futility—set in, employees and their productivity suffer. It makes sense why that happens. More specifically, think of emotional exhaustion as tiring to your bones. Not just, "this was a particularly long season" or navigating a big push to a deadline. Emotional exhaustion is, "I just can't seem to rest enough," either when a big deadline is looming or on any given Wednesday. I often hear people say, "I don't know what's wrong with me? In my PJs by 6 PM, I can sleep for 12 hours and still wake up tired." Or conversely, "I'm so exhausted. How come I can't sleep?" Remember earlier when we talked about being in a heightened state of arousal? It takes an incredible amount of internal resources for your body to be ready to "fight" or be "on" at any given moment. And here we are: In addition to all the other stresses that were coming before this pandemic hit, so many of us (read: all of us) have been in a heightened state of arousal for years. We're so irritable and "chippy"—wars are erupting and there is very little reprieve before the "next thing" hits, it seems. No wonder we're tired.

The second identified cost, as Freudenberger saw it, is the idea of depersonalization or losing compassion for others as a consequence of this burnout experience. So many of us are in the business of serving other humans. And at one point, we liked people. I can't tell you how many times lately I've heard (and have said myself), "I don't even like people." Or I find myself judging everyone I come across more superficially than I ever remember. "What the hell is wrong with that guy?" "Who buys a purple Jeep anyway?" Our tolerance, empathy, and kindness are becoming less and less accessible, primarily because we're all just so emotionally exhausted—an exhaustion that renders any of those most vulnerable emotions unavailable.

Finally, the third component of this burnout debacle is a decreased sense of accomplishment in those of us in the workforce. It's like our "give a shit" is broken. This is the one that, to me, feels the most contagious. Those around you say things like "What's the point?" and you start to wonder about that, too. If you've ever said (or thought), "You're leaving at 3? Well then fuck it, I'm out of here, too," or "I don't owe this place anything"—this futility thing has settled in.

If there are a significant number of employees in any given organization who are "burned out," imagine what that does to productivity, innovation, and creativity. The specific work that we do matters far less than the culture in which we do it. No doubt, within those professions that are more physically dangerous or where the opportunities for exposure to trauma are part of the job, the necessity for a safe place to land in a supportive integrated workplace culture becomes even more important. But ironically, it's often in organizations where the stress is high that divisiveness becomes so much a part of the culture. In fact, a guy named Figley[9] further highlighted the seemingly more specific burnout experienced in the helping professions and called it "compassion fatigue." He identified it as the "cost of caring" for others' emotional pain. This concept makes particular sense to me. As a mom, a psychologist, and a holder of many broken stories, compassion fatigue felt right when I read about it. It was only then that I started to question how it was that I had lost my love for people. How did I get tired of wanting to care for and care about people? Was there only so much that we had in our hearts to give away? See, this didn't quite make sense to me until I read Gabor Maté's *The Myth of Normal*,[10] refuting the concept of compassion fatigue. He said, there's no such thing as "compassion fatigue"—we don't get tired of the very thing we are wired for: connection. See, it isn't the caring that you get tired of. No one gets tired of caring, of serving, of walking others home. We get tired when we forget just how much we matter. When those we are serving can't or don't acknowledge us. When we get too tired to acknowledge each other. When we don't feel seen. When we don't shift the focus, at least from time to time, from them to us.

BALANCE IS BULLSHIT

Suggestions on how to achieve the elusive work-life balance are everywhere. (By the way, I think that balance is unachievable bullshit.) Once again, there's the desire to "fix"—to get to the strategies and suggestions part of how to deal with a problem instead of understanding and just sitting with the dynamics of many of our workplace cultures that bust up our collective mental health. I can tell you that when work is a safe, engaged, inclusive place, you will have a remarkably better shot at being well, even in the most physically and emotionally exhausting environments. An increasing body of research shows that work and employment aren't only drivers of happiness, but that happiness can itself help to shape job market outcomes, productivity, and even firm performance.[11] Being happy at work thus isn't just a personal matter; it's also an economic one and a socially important lifesaver.

The question is: Does workplace culture really fuck us up that bad? For the sake of understanding just how impactful where you work and how you're treated can be, I want to take a bit of a detour into a particular profession that presents the perfect paradox of a highly traumatic, much-needed service coupled with a culture that's historically not good at emotions. We have long been able to ascribe the level of stress that accompanies specific professions and thus indicates your predetermined wellness. Let's do a quick review of a popular profession where trauma and work frequently collide, and let's look at what happens when there isn't the infrastructure in place to look after your own.

THE ULTIMATE HUMAN WALKERS: FIRST RESPONDERS

If you're a first responder—defined as someone who has taken a job, paid or voluntary, to help anyone in a time of great distress (e.g., a nurse, physician, police officer, firefighter, emergency medical responder, corrections officer, 911 dispatcher, mental health worker, funeral director), you have agreed to do some of the most important work on the planet. You're in charge of other humans when they're at their most dysregulated, to keep them safe in that dysregulated state, and, ideally, to walk them home. If you're married to, gave birth to, or simply love a first responder—this job is always, in all ways, a family commitment.

I've spent a lot of time with first responders in my career, particularly police officers. In fact, I was a civilian member of our national police force for nearly two years before entering grad school. There was a (thankfully brief) period when I was convinced I would be an incredible police officer. A well-timed (for me) hiring freeze by the police force (and a subsequent realization that I don't take direction well) curbed that dream. I was amazed, even back then, that first responders, particularly police officers whose only job, truly, is to assist emotionally dysregulated people, had very little infrastructure built into their organizations to regulate the emotions of their employees. Suicide rates among police officers across North America continue to rise.[12;13] The divorce rates within these professions are significant although seemingly hard to measure, and domestic violence is often considered underreported.[14;15;16] The vast majority (read: *all*) of the focus was on how to contain the behavior of the people first responders serve. Further, to this day, there is no formalized program for first-responder spouses. And let me remind us all, you are only as okay as the people who hold you.

As we talked about in chapter 4, traumatic experiences can significantly debilitate the relationships in your life. In many first-responder worlds, encoding an experience in terror is not just something that might happen. Depending on your specific role, traumatic experiences can happen multiple times a shift. In fact, it's suggested that the average citizen experiences a terror-inducing situation two to three times in their life. As you can imagine, first responders, particularly police, fire, and other emergency services responders (nurses, physicians, and dispatchers), experience traumatic situations at least that many times in a single shift. Not surprisingly, researchers note a significant connection between traumatic event exposures and all mental health disorders.[17;18]

I've sat with police chiefs, fire captains, and other senior leaders who have tried to understand how to recruit better, to pick the ones who won't get "the PTSD" or to find the ones who won't be as likely to encode experiences in terror. Now, I think that's absurd. Trauma is unpredictable; what we experience and how we're going to encode it on any day can't be predetermined. What do we do when, not if, a brutal shift happens? What are the systems in place to regulate employees so that the body can begin to process and integrate those experiences? The issue isn't the work per se, because we're wired to do all the hard things in this world. It's what we do with the experiences that matters. And when there isn't anywhere to put the huge emotions often associated with traumatic experiences, they can turn you ugly. When you serve dysregulated people—and those who experience dysregulation most often are those who have been marginalized—you create the breeding ground for racism, discrimination, and prejudice.[19;20]

WHEN YOUR JOB IS TRAUMA

Unprocessed big emotion sometimes gets stuck. It can then keep you up at night, give you bad dreams, have you experience flashbacks as though you were still at the scene, make you irritable, and understandably fuck with your concentration. It's not that you're not tough enough to handle it. Not that you should have been better. Not that you should have necessarily done anything differently. The experience itself tends to be far less important than how the circumstances were encoded and when you attend to the consequences or fallout from that experience. Without question, post-traumatic stress disorder is not a mental illness—it is a psychological injury. Just like a physical injury, the sooner we address it, the better the prognosis becomes.

Let me give you an analogy. Let's say you are the captain of the local rugby team; a tough sport, where your team's job is to move the ball down the field, destroying anyone who stands in your way with a tackle or a head grab. You're the star of this team; the fans and your teammates love you. You're dependable, you're strong, you're fit, you take on challenges, you can handle anything. You've often said, "Put me in, I got it. I want to be the one in the last two minutes of the game." Most of all, you pride yourself on how tough you are and how weak you're not. Tears are for babies.

So, let's pretend you're in that big game and in a scrum. And in the mess of it all, somebody steps on your leg and there is instant, crushing pain. In fact, for a brief moment, your kneecap moves around to the back of your leg, just temporarily. It's bad, and you know it. But you're the tough one. And no one is allowed to see it because it's not the culture on this team, you're the leader here, it's the big game, and be damned if you're going down. So, you grab that kneecap, before anyone can see, and you shove it back into place. Now, as an aside, I am not even sure if it's anatomically possible to move your patella like this, but stick with me. Most everyone says, "Holy shit! Are you okay?" (Fuck. They did notice.) There's some fear and panic. You, on the other hand, are not the weak one, remember? You say, "I'm good. It's fine." And to demonstrate to your crew just how fine you are, you get up and "walk it off." You might even march around a little and add a "Let's go!" to prove your point.

Now, in your head you start thinking, "Fuck, this hurts. I have to get out of here before anyone knows." And you might even start to panic a little, and you head home. In the next few days, it's so painful. You take some painkillers and just hope the swelling subsides. In the weeks that follow, you "push through the pain," although you're not sleeping great because it keeps you up at night. You're back on the pitch, you show up for your team, but people start asking if you're okay. So much so that this starts to piss you off. You're irritable, and that sleeping thing is becoming harder. You're trying to walk "normal," so everyone stops (fucking) asking. But it hurts. At the end of the day, after practice, it really hurts, so you start to have a drink or two before bed, just to "settle the nerves." A little doesn't work anymore after a few weeks. So you start to drink a little more and add some pills into the mix. You're not as good as you used to be on the field (obviously) and that pisses you off, too. The coach starts to sit you. A lot. You start fighting with people because you were "the star," and now everybody thinks you're not. And you wake up one day, mad, exhausted, hating everybody, and in so much pain.

Now, in this little scenario, let's assume this is where you and I meet. I want you to consider for a second that, often, this is exactly how emotional injuries occur. And sometimes people come into my office and say, "I think something's wrong. I'm irritable and pissed off all the time. My marriage is falling apart. I hate my job, and my previously beloved teammates are assholes." But you've never talked about that day on the pitch, you've never told anyone that your patella spent some time at the back of your leg. You can imagine that if we jumped to treating the symptoms here, I'd maybe suggest you get more painkillers; maybe get you to practice some gratitude, journal, drink more water, and get rest. How effective do you think that would be?

So instead I'll likely ask you to tell me more, until we can get to your story. Eventually, you tell me about that day on the field, and I ask if I can see your knee. At first you say no, asking if there's anything else we can do to make it better—like maybe a brace or something. Now, of course we can do those things, but you and I likely both know, even if you're unable to admit it, we're going to have to take a look at that knee if we ever want to figure this out. Together, we look. Indeed, your patella is nowhere near where it should be, and in the many months since this has happened, it's not healed well.

Here's the deal. Hypothetically, of course, we must reset this leg. So many times, at this point, "the work" of feeling it all becomes difficult. And it hurts. With traumatic injuries, I'm far less interested in the logistics of what happened on the field—like where the bodies were lying, or how, logistically, someone didn't execute a call correctly. I'm much more interested in how it felt. And then stories, often in our human services professions, are filled with moments on scene or in treatment rooms where the kid you were serving had jammies just like your baby at home. Or you were first on scene with no backup, and you encoded the whole thing in terror, but never, ever talked about it—most especially, you never talked about the feeling. Or how now, once you talk about it, you realize the reason you hate filling up your car with gasoline is that the smell takes you back to the scene of that fire where you didn't realize there was a gas can in the corner. And it exploded. And (most importantly), you've felt nothing ever since but shame and stupidity for "missing it."

Back to the patella for a second. You might say to me, "Doc, now that we've talked about it, are we good?" Oh, friend, I wish it were that easy. Now there's physio and walking again a bit differently. You're frustrated with me, because you'll say, "I thought this was supposed to get better." And I'll remind you that two months ago, you couldn't walk straight, and now you can. You might say to me, "Yeah, but I used to be able to run down the whole field while tackling six different people, dammit!" See, the question I often get asked is, "Will it ever be the same again?" And here's the deal. No, you won't ever be the same. None of us are the same today as we were yesterday. All our experiences change us somehow. The key is how we make sense of it all.

Emotional injuries, when our mental health is gravely affected, can be so isolating. The stigma remains the biggest, baddest barrier that debilitates people, sometimes more than the injury itself. This is exacerbated in the world of first responders because the culture is not conducive to addressing the hard things. This is further perpetuated by the very call of the job—which is to serve other people who need help. We (they) feel so much more competent when we can "fix" someone else.

PROCESSING THE EMOTIONS OF THE JOB

For what it's worth, I can tell you that addressing emotional illness will not make you "soft." You won't "lose skills on scene" if you put the hard stuff somewhere, sometimes. In fact, the more you address the emotions away from the scene, the sharper you are on scene. Historically, critical incident stress debriefings were introduced to mitigate this problem. However, often they're not done at all. And if they're done but are poorly executed, that can be particularly damaging.[21] In fact, one phenomenal former police officer told me, after 13 years in the field and a debilitating PTSD diagnosis, "Not even once—not even once did we have a conversation about unpacking what happened on shift. Not even once."

In their groundbreaking book *Burnout: The Secret to Unlocking the Stress Cycle*,[22] the Nagoski sisters make it clear that exhaustion happens when we get stuck in the emotion. In fact, this might be one of my favorite lines: "Just because you've dealt with the stressor doesn't mean you've dealt with the stress." Just because we make it to the weekend or the next holiday or retirement or the file finally being closed or the sadistic, racist, sexist, boss we had no longer being at the helm, it doesn't mean the weight of everything we carried to get there also suddenly disappears. Often, in fact, it's when things slow down—or our bodies just start to slow down for us because they can no longer handle the weight of it all—that stuff gets harder. It changes how we think and what we think about, and it can even significantly impact our *ability* to think.

Even after spending the first part of this very honored career of mine stepping into some of the most traumatic stories of others, I maintain that I don't think it's the job itself that is the most predictive of the unhealthiest among us. I'm starting to be clear that the jobs that are most beneficial to mental health can't really be specified by profession, title, or industry because a lot depends on personal standards and cultures. If you're doing some of the most intense and stressful work, you can do it beautifully and with all the heart in the world if you're surrounded by a team of (mostly) regulated people. Regardless of pay, physical safety, and hours, you can do hard things.

Mental health is not just a human resources issue; it's also an equity, diversity, and inclusion issue. Mental health needs to be considered through an intersectional lens. This means that HR departments or check-the-box solutions like employee assistance programs are not enough to address the nuances of mental health or drive change, nor will mental health policies alone solve the problem. Regardless of how robust a company's benefits are, it is the workplace culture that ultimately reduces stigma and empowers employees to use those benefits without fear of retribution. Workplaces where there is joy within the culture is a huge sign that things are going well.

Here's what I know: When you do good work, you will have bad days. It's not if, it's when. And here's the other stupid truth: Even if you do all the preparation in the world, it still doesn't ward off the pain when the hard things happen at work. Or when rejection or criticism is high and even the people you love the most don't seem to notice just how fucking hard you're working at this job. See, contrary to our primitive response to the pain, the trick is not to avoid it and play small, but instead know that bravery will require you to step in with your whole heart, especially when you can't predict the outcome. If you're going to give it away, it's going to get broken. Maybe the most important question is, what's our plan to catch you when, not if, you fall? This life is messy, particularly when we're navigating marriage, sometimes kids, and careers. There is a cost when we don't focus on us, and it sometimes looks like trauma. When we spend enough time in those disconnected places, there will be significant prices to pay. So, once again, before we jump into how we address it, let's make sure we've officially ripped your soul out.

BRINGING IT BACK HOME

The cultures within the places we go when we spend time away from our families to earn a living are becoming profoundly important to consider when we want to improve our relationships. So many more of us work outside the home today, more than ever (and working remotely from home comes with even more challenges), and that number is not going to decrease. One of the most important investments we may make is considering how we can create more connections between these two historically very separate entities. If the people we love aren't okay, we will not perform well at work for long. Organizations that look after their people and allow them to stay connected to their families too, create healthy, productive cultures. When that doesn't happen, relationships within those systems start to disintegrate. We end up in a war of disconnection. And we may just be closer to that than we think. Although we often call for systemic or policy change at the senior leadership levels, I promise you that change happens more quickly when you consider the impact of a few small things. For example:

1. What team is one of the best at work or in a volunteer role that you've been a part of—and what made it so great?
2. How often, in your community, are people set up to acknowledge the first responders who serve in your hospitals or nonprofits?
3. What one thing can you do tomorrow for the staff you work with or a team in your community that might bring some joy? (Examples: leaving notes on their cars, bringing a high-quality charcuterie board to the staffroom, or leaving a chalk message on the front steps of the office.) What might this gesture mean for those who work there?

CHAPTER SIX

The Dawn of Disconnect

THE UNFUCKINGBELIEVEABLE COSTS OF COLONIZATION, RACISM, AND MARGINALIZATION

A word of caution before we talk about where disconnection originated: This chapter contains particularly difficult content. I have written it in consultation and under the advisement of those who know so much more than I do, including, among others, Sarah Adomako-Ansah, educator in residence at the Canadian Museum for Human Rights. For those of you who are Indigenous or racialized, colonization and racism aren't theoretical; the impacts are continually felt daily. And if you are a settler, as I am, you may also experience sadness, guilt, shame, anger, or confusion as you read this chapter. Although exploring how we got here is critical, how we listen, do better, and be better is the goal. But you can't address what you won't acknowledge. If you're up for it, let's dive in.

How did we get here? How the fuck did we get here? I don't think we ask that question nearly enough. We're so committed to the fix. So committed to measuring compliance and productivity that we forget to ask why some people can't show up. Why some people have never felt seen and, in turn, will not be able truly to see others. How come some people default to fucking up every relationship they've ever been in? We quite often land on all the things they're not: motivated enough, caring enough; or clearly, they're assholes. Now listen, all that might be true, but I can tell you this—there's always a story. And we mix up our "stories" with excuses all the time. Let's, for at least one chapter, put aside the measurement or judgment of a behavior or an outcome and dive a little deeper into why, and how, we got to a place where we treat people so remarkably unequally and then wonder why we have predictably different outcomes.

This is the final chapter in this section, and it's the one that scares me the most. It's the culmination of the most difficult but necessary conversations I feel the least prepared to have. It's easier not to have this conversation, mostly because it's so easy to get it "wrong." There's so much riding on truly seeing people who have been marginalized, been disrespected, or experienced genocide, because the trust in the goodness of humanity has, to some degree, been shattered. The irony of a privileged white girl writing these words doesn't escape me. Where I land, however, is considering that we would never expect the ones who have suffered the most to teach the ones who did the hurting how to help them heal. It is the job of privileged people to do the work. So, for all the ways I might get it wrong, for all the things you might notice I have yet to learn and unlearn in this chapter in particular, what I have learned for sure is staying silent is not an option. This chapter, for me, is all about creating a long overdue space for the things so many of us— particularly those who are privileged—spend a lot of time hoping either don't exist or are simply "not as bad as some people say."

DARKEST AFTER THE DAWN

The truth is, the dawn of disconnect—where the deepest seeds of disconnect were first planted—was in the erroneous belief that some humans are better than others. Despite the fact that we all start in exactly the same place—the wombs of our mothers—somehow, somewhere, it was decided that certain characteristics made some of those with heartbeats better than others. That somewhere is what we refer to as colonization, built from the theory that is colonialism. Here's my take on the theory that became the epitome of being unseen.

THE ROOT OF MANY EVILS: COLONIALISM

Colonialism is the theory that embodies this belief: We are superior to everyone else, so that means we have the right to take over the land of another and run it for our own benefit. Colonization is then acting out that theory—the sending of our (superior) people to physically take the land away from their (inferior) people and run it for the benefit of our (superior) people while relegating their (inferior) people to subservient and secondary roles (that is, if our [superior] people don't simply kill off or eliminate their [inferior] people).

Colonization has occurred throughout time—one nation tries to possess another nation and assimilate its citizens to the colonizer's ways, norms, and culture. Consider the sheer scale and its ongoing global impacts by European (including British) nations that colonized much of the world and embedded beliefs that will take far beyond our lifetimes to unlearn. In fact, European colonization changed the way the entire world functions. The motivations for the first waves of colonial expansion have been summed up as God, gold, and glory: God, because missionaries felt it was their moral duty to spread Christianity, and they believed a higher power would reward them for saving the souls of colonial subjects; gold, because colonizers would exploit resources of other countries in order to bolster their own economies; and glory, since

European nations would often compete with one another over the glory of attaining the greatest number of colonies.[1]

The intense competition between major European powers led to increased exploration, the building of trade networks, and a scramble for colonies. It was the Portuguese, in the late 1400s, who began direct encounters with the peoples of coastal West and Central Africa, and by the 1500s they had seized several key Asian ports. Meanwhile, Spanish fleets led by the often-lauded Christopher Columbus discovered a huge landmass to the west, soon to be named America. Columbus had hoped to find the sea route to China and Southeast Asia, and to introduce Christianity into these distant realms. Both the Portuguese and the Spanish promised the Pope to evangelize and colonize the "heathen" peoples they encountered. In Canada, colonialism moved across the country from east to west, and, noticeably, eastern Indigenous communities were and are affected differently; however, much of the "history" gets taught as a singular experience.

Most problematically, North American history is often taught from the perspective of the dominant culture—the colonizer's perspective, devoid of any (or light on, at best) acknowledgment of the racist policies and actions embedded within the government practices. I, as one example, got my PhD in this country and I have no recollection of learning terms like "the 60s scoop" or the name Turtle Island, or that Columbus was anything but a hero. As a very brief summary, some of the policies that were never taught extensively in mainstream education include the genocide of Indigenous Peoples and the continued breaking of numerous treaties with First Nations, Inuit, and Métis Peoples; the development of the Indian residential school system in Canada—with the intent of a cultural genocide; internment of American and Canadian citizens of Japanese descent during World War II;

constitutional encoding of enslavement of Africans and all others until the 13th Amendment was instated in the United States; the post-13th Amendment imposition of Jim Crow and Sundown laws; and racial profiling of Latinx, African Americans, Indigenous Peoples, and other people of color. The consequences of these policies continue to perpetuate every aspect of society today; however, the cause of those consequences have never been made clear. And you can't address, or even understand, let alone have empathy for what you don't acknowledge. You can't reconcile anything fully if you don't have the truth.

RACISM

European colonizers who benefited in advancements more quickly than other parts of the world also happened to be white-skinned people. White supremacy, more specifically, developed as a direct result of colonial practices, based on the egregious assumption that white people are superior to those of other races and thus should dominate them. Its purpose is the maintenance and defense of a system of wealth, power, and privilege. More specifically, white supremacy has roots in the now-discredited doctrine of scientific racism—the claim that there was "data" to suggest white people were better, smarter, more pure; thus, a key justification for colonialism. It developed over multiple generations, and we have only begun the work of undoing a system of understanding that is so embedded in every institution we're currently a part of. White supremacy is a global sociopolitical imagination of human dominance. In this sense, it's simultaneously an ideological, epistemological, cultural, institutional, militarized, and aesthetic structuring of power, coercion, and social identity.[2] It's powerful. It's real. And it's so often not considered as the impetus for so many ideologies created in a world that no longer exists (and, in fact, never did).

See, colonization was built on racism. Race is a social construct and not a biological reality. Race is a human-invented, shorthand term used to describe and categorize people into various social groups based on characteristics like skin color, physical features, and genetic heredity. Race, as we've come to understand here, while not a valid biological concept, is a social construction that gives or denies benefits and privileges. The term "race," used infrequently before the 1500s, was used to identify groups of people with a kinship or group connection. The modern-day use of the term "race" is a human invention. In fact, human DNA is 99.9 percent identical between all humans, and after that there is even less variation between societally determined racial groups than there is within them. We are, absolutely, way more alike than we are different.

Just because something is a social construct doesn't mean it isn't "real" in terms of its impact on people's everyday lives. In fact, racism does not exist without trauma. In the country where I am sitting, writing these words, Indigenous Peoples were identified as savages and wards of the state. As settlers came and governments were built, Indigenous Peoples' presence and resistance to assimilation created the "Indian problem" that worked against normalizing a story of Canada as a champion of human rights and a progressive nation.

Further, an extensive residential school system was developed by the Canadian government and administered by churches that had the nominal objective of educating Indigenous children but also the more damaging and equally explicit objectives of indoctrinating them into Euro-Canadian and Christian ways of living and assimilating them into mainstream white Canadian society. I have had the humbling honor of being in the presence of survivors of the residential school system, where the deep-rooted trauma is evident in the horrific stories some of them are brave enough to tell. Children four years old and up were forced from their homes to these institutions, where many were physically, sexually, and emotionally abused in an attempt at cultural genocide. The last Indian residential school was closed in Saskatchewan in 1996.[3] And as recently as within months of writing these words, hundreds of unmarked graves of the children who did not survive (because of untreated illnesses and/or abuse or neglect) their experiences at these institutions are still being recovered across North America.[4,5] In fact, it wasn't until 2015 that a report was provided to the Canadian federal government and the public. The final report of the Truth and Reconciliation Commission of Canada established calls for 94 actions toward restoring a balanced relationship between Indigenous Peoples and settler communities in this country. It's so clear that reconciliation requires a commitment from non-Indigenous people to understand the past, recognize treaty agreements, build equitable relationships, and support the restoration of Indigenous Peoples' languages and culture. Important work is still needed, because as of June 30, 2021, only 14 calls to action have been completed, while 23 are in progress with projects underway, 37 are in progress with projects proposed, and 20 have yet to be started.[6]

Racism remains the construct, integrating itself into behaviors of intolerance, prejudice, alienation, criminalization, and discrimination. Although race is a false category, theories of racial superiority and discrimination remain ingrained and often unchallenged. In fact, almost all cognitive biases, both conscious and unconscious, influence our perception of race and can be linked to the perpetuation of racism.[7] For example, the in-group bias, which is where we favor people who look like us and see out-groups as having less favorable attributes, is often linked with discriminatory behavior. And researchers have shown that an "us versus them" mentality increases the likelihood of out-group prejudices to develop. See, human brains are hardwired to take shortcuts when processing information to make decisions, resulting in "systematic thinking errors" or unconscious bias.[8] When it comes to influencing our decisions and judgments about people, cognitive or unconscious bias is universally recognized to play a role in unequal outcomes for people of color.[9] It unfortunately stands to reason then that, if there is a long-standing history of what is the most acceptable when it comes to a certain standard of human, those who do not fit within that certain standard would experience significantly less privilege than those who do. Those on the outside have been identified as "marginalized."

MARGINALIZATION

Marginalized communities are those excluded from mainstream social, economic, educational, and/or cultural life. Largely, marginalization falls into three main types—social, economic, and political—and can include, but is not limited to, groups excluded because of race, gender identity, sexual orientation, age, physical ability, language, and/or immigration status. Those in the "in group," not living at the fringes but closer to the center, where the good things come in abundance, are often said to have privilege.

The word "privilege" comes from the Latin *privilegium*, meaning a law for just one person, entailing benefits enjoyed by an individual or group beyond what's available to others. Within American and other Western societies, these privileged social identities—of people who have historically occupied positions of dominance over others—include white, male, able-bodied, straight, Christian, and those who have money or own property.[10] The research to support this list is irrefutable, and, instead of "proving" that list (which is so easy to do), I think a better use of our time is to review (briefly) the costs of not being in the in-group and, more profoundly, the cumulative effect of intersectionality (in other words, the more of the privileged categories you don't fit into, the more difficult your life undoubtedly will be).

Here's how I think about it sometimes: You can't judge people at the finish line until you've assessed where they started. When I look at people who I've shared the stage with or sat down in meetings with, I'm interested in their story. Because even though we may be in a similar space, I had a lot of things in my favor when I started this human race: I'm white, straight, able-bodied, middle to upper class. I had a huge head start. As author and bad-ass feminist Glennon Doyle wrote, I "started on third base." If you look at someone who stands on a stage, speaks, writes, creates a platform, but did not start in the same place of privilege, consider how much harder and faster they've had to work to get to a similar place in life. I don't think it's good or bad that we're both here. It means that if you truly want to appreciate your head start, you will use it for good.

Just for the record, does that mean white, straight, able-bodied people don't struggle? That's not what I'm saying. Does it mean that some Black, trans, disabled people haven't had it "easier" than some white people? Well, I promise you that, on the average, it would be extremely difficult to find data to support that. And even if we did, we're not talking about a single experience. I am most concerned about what it looks like for the whole. For this community. For people who need to be acknowledged and seen, and just whose job that might be.

When we consider all the ways that trauma has shown up in our understanding of humans—trauma along the lines of bias and racism and living in such a place of divisiveness—it's no surprise that at the heart of this place of disconnect are things like addiction and a massive toll on our collective mental health. When you've survived multiple generations of racism, marginalization, abuse, and neglect, where are your eyes? How difficult might it be to see and be seen? How inaccessible, understandably, are the most vulnerable parts of the soul?

I want to unpack the so-often-lumped-together addiction and mental health grouping into two very different things. One is a way of coping—that's addiction. And the other can be a clinical diagnosis that may be the outcome of disconnect or trauma—a havoc wreaked on your mental health. So, let's dive into both those now, starting first with the numbing attempt to manage the unprocessed emotions that often leads to the disconnect in our relationships: addiction.

THE WELCOME NUMB OF ADDICTION

Addiction is an inability to stop using a substance or engaging in a behavior, even though it's causing psychological, physical, and often relational harm. I think about addiction like this: When the trauma gets too much and it becomes too hard to step into the world again and again and again, we use substances to numb reality. Sometimes it feels good to just take a break every so often. However, when escaping the present feels better than staying where you're at, the substance or the behavior that takes you to that place of reprieve becomes very attractive. And the more you tend to numb, especially when it starts to interfere with your daily functioning, use becomes an addiction. Among Americans ages 12 years and older, 31.9 million are current illegal drug users ;[11] and if alcohol and tobacco are included, 60.2 percent of Americans ages 12 years and older currently abuse those drugs. Substance use of all kinds typically becomes worse in times of depression and war. Emotions are often too heavy to bear, particularly when we have no reprieve. I wish you could selectively numb; however, when you're numbing all the "bad" stuff, you also miss out on all the good stuff and lose your ability to stay vulnerably connected in your relationships.

There is a large consensus that addictive behavior is increasing, most notably since the onset of the pandemic.[12] See, it makes sense when we consider what we know: Human beings crave connection, bonding, and love. When meaningful connection is missing from our lives, an addiction may begin to fill the void. One of my favorite writers on this subject is British journalist Johann Hari, who said that trying to eliminate addictive substances from society, as the "war on drugs" attempts to do, is ultimately a losing strategy because it avoids the root problem—a lack of social connection. "There is an alternative. You can build a system that is designed to help drug addicts to reconnect with the world—and so leave behind their addictions."[13]

Addiction was once viewed as an unsavory fringe disease, tethered to substances with killer withdrawal symptoms, such as alcohol and opium. But now the scope of what humans can be addicted to seems to have snowballed, from sugar to shopping to sex to social media. Neuroscience has now largely accepted that it's the same brain chemical, dopamine, driving these cravings;[14] however, as Hari[15] has pointed out, the answer to addiction is not sobriety. It's connection.

UNSEEN

I'm reminded of Jake (we will call him), a client who was once "assigned" to me. His only child, nine-year-old Noah, had been placed in foster care following allegations against Jake of emotional abuse and neglect. Noah's mom was in jail. It was my job to supervise the visits between Jake and Noah and provide an opinion to the court about whether Jake had the capacity to care for his son full time. Jake was in his 30s, had a trauma history that included being abandoned by his mom at 14, and had been physically abused by his father and uncles most of his life. He had not completed high school, had a criminal record, and had used every legal and illegal substance available. And Jake loved his son desperately.

The direction from the agency was to be very careful and cautious during the visits; in fact, having a police presence was recommended, as Jake had a history of "extreme violence." He was understandably so (fucking) mad that he needed some woman to sit with him and watch him visit his kid. I understood that completely and, after weighing my options, I decided to forgo police presence. After a failed first meeting where Jake didn't show (he got his "times wrong"), Jake was given another time, was directed to "not be late," bring a "healthy snack" for his son, and appear "appropriate" during the visit (in an apparent test to demonstrate his ability to care for his son). A breaking of any of these "rules" was grounds to cancel the visit, understandably in an effort to protect the child, and often to "teach a lesson" to the uncompliant parent. As I sat with Noah, who was excited to see his dad but cautiously unoptimistic because Jake was often unreliable, I saw him brighten when he heard his dad's truck pull up outside the office. Jake was 33 minutes late.

When I went outside to meet Jake first, I couldn't help but notice he had driven his 18-wheel "work truck" into town, taking up most of the block. He ran toward me, carrying a McDonald's bag. "I'm so fucking sorry, ma'am. I know I'm late. My pickup broke down and I had to bring my work truck. And I didn't have time to make the healthy snack—but I got him a burger." As I got closer to Jake, his eyes were bloodshot and he smelled like he hadn't showered in some time. I caught his eye and said, "Please tell me there's a cheeseburger in that bag." I saw his shoulders drop, and he told me, "It is! Noah's favorite." I said, "You sure know your boy, Dad. He's excited to see you. Let's head inside."

Jake and Noah did so well that day. Jake needed a couple of smoke breaks when we got to talking about some of the things you should discuss with your nine-year-old, and maybe some things you shouldn't. When it was time to leave that small room, which was filled with stupid toys neither of them were familiar with, both of them were sad. They hugged, and I helped Noah into the car of the driver who would take him back to his foster home. When I came back to see Jake off, he looked like a little boy himself, sitting on the hard standard-issue couch. As he got up to leave, I asked, "You up for a hug, Dad?" I could smell the marijuana and the grease and gasoline from his job, and I don't think I have hugged a human tighter. He dissolved into tears. "Jody, I love him. More than anything in my life. I don't know how to do this shit. No one taught me. I know I fuck it up sometimes. But I don't know if I could ever live without him." After that, Jake never missed another visit. He was never late, and I believe he was sober every time.

Two months later, after talking it through with him first, I stood in a court of law and explained that Jake likely didn't have the means necessary to care for his child full time; however, it was imperative (in my opinion) that he see him regularly. In this case, which sadly doesn't happen often, there was a family member, Noah's aunt, who agreed to be the full-time guardian, and Jake was granted the permission to remain active in Noah's life. I haven't seen them for some time, but I understand (because these ones never leave your heart) that Noah is about to graduate Grade 12 and Jake will be there. Jake was so right. You can't give away something you've never received. Jake lived in the margins his whole life and didn't have many "skills" expected of him, but he loved his son just like every parent I've ever met. When you feel like you've failed the people who matter most to you in this world—or when they repeatedly fail you—that reality is sometimes brutally difficult to tolerate. So, you don't. That's addiction.

A MENTAL HEALTH CRISIS

Different from addiction, although often intertwined, is mental illness—and that link is understandable. When we are disconnected and largely unwitnessed in our human experience, whether because of our belief that we have failed, mental illness, the color of our skin, or the intersectionality of these things, the emotional dysregulatory costs leave us disappointed in ourselves and unable to reconnect to the thing we need the most: each other. And as you can imagine, both addiction and mental illness disproportionately plague those who are marginalized. Emotional illness, for the first time in our history, is killing us at a faster rate than physical illness.[16] Essentially, things like anxiety and depression (which can often lead to suicide) are the leading cause of death, even exceeding heart and stroke or cancer. When I first read this statistic, it became, for me, the flagship, the unmistakable beacon, flare, and raging storm, that would suggest something has to change. We're missing something when numbers start to look increasingly dire. For instance, during the pandemic, about four in 10 adults in the United States reported symptoms of anxiety or depressive disorder, up from one in 10 adults who reported these symptoms from January to June 2019.[17]

More specifically, young adults have experienced several pandemic-related consequences that may contribute to poor mental health. When we consider university closures and loss of income, this may perhaps be the most affected subgroup. Further, the pandemic has disproportionately affected the health of communities of color. Non-Hispanic Black adults and Hispanic or Latinx adults are more likely to report symptoms of anxiety and/ or depressive disorder than non-Hispanic white adults. Historically, and as an additional concern, communities of color have faced challenges accessing mental health care. The next most significantly affected cohort appears to be women, particularly mothers. Researchers during the pandemic pointed to concerns around poor mental health and well-being for children and their parents, particularly mothers, as many are experiencing challenges with school closures and lack of childcare. Women with children are more likely to report symptoms of anxiety and/or depressive disorder than are men with children.[18]

I think we often get confused when we use words like "anxiety" and "depression" when considering what it means to have a clinical experience with one of these disorders. There's a big difference between sadness and depression. Sadness is common but not an essential feature of depression; sadness is an emotion that we all feel sometimes. Clinical depression, on the other hand, and in fact any illness that is defined as clinical, significantly debilitates your functioning. Worrying and anxiety are not the same thing. There will be times when we feel anxious or sad about things, but that doesn't mean we are clinically anxious or depressed. As we've discovered, how we name things matters. How we understand our experiences will directly impact the way we respond. Understanding why is critical.

In short, one of the most significant ramifications of the decline in our mental health can be death by suicide. "Suicide" is one of the most horrific words I know. It means different things to different people, I suppose. But the sheer pain associated with those considering ending their own life, and for those left behind, continues to be one of the heaviest burdens in this world. And it's not an uncommon experience. In fact, over 700,000 people die by suicide in the world each year,[19] which is roughly 1,917 deaths every day. In Canada, in a study of people 15 years and older, those who are lesbian, gay, and bisexual are more likely to experience depression, anxiety, suicidality, and substance abuse than their heterosexual counterparts. In the United States, suicide is the second leading cause of death for 10- to 34-year-old Americans, while the highest rate of death by suicide is experienced by middle-aged men.[20] Specifically, males die by suicide three and a half times more often than women, and Indigenous men and Indigenous youth are 10 times more at risk.[21] This statistic is one I often talk about when speaking to members of male-dominated occupations—like our oil and gas industries and corporate entities, agriculture, sports organizations, and first responders. Why are middle-aged men the ones who are dying most by suicide? I think this finding lends significant support to what we talked about in our first section—that a scarcity of emotional language and expression is deadly.

DEEP BREATH

When I think about "what now," at first it all feels like too much (even from this place of privilege). And then I think about how grateful I am to be alive at a time when real, systemic awareness and acknowledgment might just be taking hold. Reducing the stigma of mental illness is an increasingly more common conversation. And books about race and anti-racism have dominated bestseller lists, bringing to prominence authors including Ibram X. Kendi, Ijeoma Oluo, Reni Eddo-Lodge, Jesse Thistle, and Robin DiAngelo. While readers learned about allyship, companies resolved to tackle racial inequality by making public statements on their social media accounts and releasing detailed action plans with their commitments to change. Further, initiatives aimed at debunking the stigma of mental health are beautifully, albeit ever-so-slowly, gaining momentum. If I've learned anything so far, however, it's that diversity is nothing without inclusion. And unlearning is never, ever, an endgame. So, deep breath with me, and know that we will keep going. We have to.

For anyone who has experienced multiple generations of oppression, what happens in this lifetime can never be fast enough. We should never have been here anyway, so how do you ever "make up for it"? The simple answer, given only from my chair, is that you don't. You can't undo what our ignorant predecessors did. Further, this narrative has led to the significant underestimation of Black and Brown wisdom, influence, and accomplishments that are often identified as "exceptions." There is a significant sense of resolve and an understanding of community that remain remarkably rich in marginalized communities—maybe out of necessity, or maybe because there is an understanding of the importance of connection that has always been there and could not be broken.

My hope for you and me sitting here together is to make inclusion and anti-racism a part of every conversation in our houses, our soccer fields, our grocery stores, and wherever we show up to work every day. That we will remain open to feedback and correction, even though our first instinct may be to armor up. That we won't partake in hard conversations just when people are watching, but mostly when they're not. That when we hear each other say things like "I can't even imagine what it must be like to be you" or "I want to take a break from it all," we are reminded that this is the epitome of privilege. Because I *can* imagine what it must be like to be refused service, to have my babies ripped from my arms, to be stuck at the bottom of a staircase and not know how to get up it, to drive on a freeway in fear of being shot—all because of the color of my skin or the ability in my body or how I identify or who I love. Ijeoma Oluo—the author of *So You Want to Talk About Race*, said, "The beauty of anti-racism is that you don't have to pretend to be free of racism to be an anti-racist. Anti-racism is the commitment to fight racism wherever you find it, including in yourself. And it's the only way forward." Indeed, it is the only way forward. And forward we will proceed. Like it's our job—because it is.

BRINGING IT BACK HOME

We all came from somewhere. Some of us are painfully aware of our history, while many others have no concept of what it took for our ancestors to navigate the sacrifices they had to make. Truths are being discovered about the false ideals that so many of our major institutions have been built on, including the narrative of our history. Remember, we don't like it when people are dysregulated. We tend to armor up and pull away. There is a significant cost to disconnection and I think that, sadly, we are just beginning to experience the effects of that cost in our homes, our workplaces, our communities, and our hospitals. When we, globally, struggle to cope with the stresses of life, which are compounded by the lack of connection to help us make sense of it all, we need a place to put down all this heaviness and emotion, if only for a while. We need each other to not look away when things get tough and to become brave enough to speak up. We can't come to terms with anything well if we aren't honest about what we're dealing with. So, leave it all here as you contemplate the things you know, and pause with these few wonderings:

1. Consider where you land on the privilege spectrum and what that has (or hasn't) meant to getting you exactly to this moment. Just notice without judgment. And breathe.
2. Why do you think it's taking so long to "unlearn" clearly refuted, previously understood "differences" between people?
3. Just consider (and name out loud if you can—even if people are sitting near you) one thing you're going to do on purpose in an active effort to explore your potential biases.

Part Two

THE ROADMAP
BACK TO
EACH OTHER

WHEN WE'RE ACKNOWLEDGED,
WE RISE

Okay. Here's where the work begins. What do we do with all these emotions and the subsequent pain they can sometimes cause—either the pains we inherited, the ones that were thrust on us by our experiences, or even the ones we're so desperately willing to step into? We will be inclined to come up with solutions and strategies to fix all this dysregulation, but this Part Two is the critical piece we so often miss. The goal, dear ones, is to eventually integrate the emotions that these experiences evoke. It's never about getting rid of our experiences (because we can't). It's truly about making sense of them so they can settle into our stories and the defenses become less necessary to protect the soul. When we process intense emotions, they don't bite us in the ass out of the blue or keep us stuck in time in an experience. The kicker: You can't go around any of it. There are no shortcuts. You have to go through it. It's the simple acknowledgment of some of the particularly dark, heavy burdens that is the key to healing. That is the work of allowing each of us to see and feel seen.

The scientific nuances of language fascinate me, but I'm no linguistics expert. For the sake of simplicity, here's what I know: language does so much more than just act as a communication tool. I can tell you what it feels like in a therapy session when you hear a deep sigh after someone finally tells their truth. Or the safety of having a good cry over a glass of wine with a soulmate who just listens. They use just the right word, a well-timed nod, or a phrase to put a name to the mess that's in your heart, and sometimes you can even physically feel the shift. Honoring the sacred nature of the story—the stories we share and the ones we hear—and knowing we've been entrusted with something valuable we should treat with respect and care. I love this skill of simply holding space because otherwise, particularly when there are cultural differences or the desire to fix or do a full-fledged narrative takeover, the result is often a clamoring lockdown of the soul. So, these next few chapters are an attempt at a deliberate slowdown—a roadmap to guide us through this process of what it truly means to acknowledge another and understand that it doesn't mean you sacrifice your worth or your beliefs along the way.

Simply acknowledging another's truth becomes particularly difficult when their experience is much unlike our own. And it seems that the more we disagree, the more we just want to fix it; get you back to a state of emotional regulation; suggest strategies or solutions or enforce our power to bring you to where we think you should be. That is the fundamental definition of behaviorism. The intention is to "make it better"; however, if we do that before truly understanding, we miss so much. I want you to consider, as we step into this next section of the book, that the most important and underused superpower in all of us is that ability to try to just "get it" first. So, deep breath, friends. We, together, have gotten through some of the hard stuff. Now let's talk about the importance of simply acknowledging—holding space for all the shit you've been through. Because when you're acknowledged, you will rise. And so will they.

CHAPTER SEVEN

Acknowledgment
THE POWER PLAY THAT CHANGES THE WHOLE GAME

I've learned that helping people move forward often first means helping them stay where they're at. So many times, we're in a rush to move on, to get over it, to feel better. This is true in grief and trauma, when we have been sideswiped by infidelity or undermined by a sudden job loss. The truth of the matter is, ironically, that sometimes we get through it faster, process it more fully, when we slow down and just feel it. In fact, some of the most sacred among us can sit in the spaces where emotional pain is almost unbearable and know there's nothing they can say or do that can fix it. There's such freedom in knowing that saying nothing at all in those most intense moments is a critical time in healing. "Holding space" sounds so easy—but it can be brutally difficult, especially when you love someone who's hurting or if you feel responsible for their pain. In recent years, we have navigated even more disconnect; however, the concept of acknowledgment has brought a richness from truly witnessing another human and facilitating growth and connection.

BUT FIRST, SIT DOWN AND SHUT UP

One of the most significant factors in witnessing another is simply listening. Seeking first to understand. Understanding the importance of listening first has taken me way longer than I'd like to admit. As a self-proclaimed articulate person, I find myself much more comfortable telling you how it is than I do learning how it is (or was) for you. In the realm of privilege, people, including me, are notoriously not good at listening. You see, we think we know the answers. We have been taught to believe we know the answers. But as time marches on in this ever-growing experience of aging, I am learning that I know less today than I've ever been aware of knowing before. The job, for so many of us, is to first sit down and shut up.

Truly, sitting down and shutting up might be one of the hardest things ever asked of anyone, because we see things from our own experiences first. Because we're most exposed to the things we know to be true, it's difficult to alter long-standing perceptions, beliefs, identities, and understandings. Being able to slow down long enough to wonder what it might be like to have an experience foreign to us, while withholding judgment—ooh-eee!—now that's a skill. The more traumatized you've become, the further damaged that ability often is. It also appears to me that as you become more divisive in your opinions, your access to the gray—that space between black and white—becomes almost unreachable. If you're so steadfastly entrenched in any belief—as evidenced by it being all you think about, know about, talk about, believe to be true—then wondering about alternative thoughts, ideas, or opinions might deserve some attention. This is different from passion (which we will talk about in the last section). Passion fuels good work; being entrenched is exhausting.

As you can appreciate, just sitting there and not saying anything often isn't enough. The actions (often even more important than the words) that follow next are the things many behaviorists don't talk a lot about: the simple, yet complicated act of acknowledging.

ACKNOWLEDGMENT: THE POWER PLAY

By formal definition, an acknowledgment is two things, both of which are identified as "acts": (1) the act of showing that you know, admit, or accept that something exists or is true; or (2) the act of recognizing someone for an achievement or experience. Both acts are so critically important in what I think it's going to take to reconnect a disconnected world. When I acknowledge somebody, when I do that act of showing that I know or accept that something exists or is true, I bring into awareness and even organize those feelings in another. Conversely, or maybe even at the same time, when I'm recognizing someone for an experience, an achievement, or an attribute, it's my witnessing of something that allows them to see themselves differently, maybe even for who they are. I have seen its physical power as people move their eyes up to meet yours after receiving a genuine acknowledgment. The definition, however, doesn't tell us the best part about genuine acknowledgments—they often benefit the acknowledger as much or even more than the recipient.

The act of acknowledgment can also serve as a powerful tool for defusing anger. It can leave anger nowhere to go, as there's no fuel for it to keep burning. In fact, it's powerful enough to soften or even melt any intense emotion. If we're lucky, that's how we uncover the sad behind the mad. It's this act of separating, pulling apart, that seems to be the necessary process for reintegration. The goal is to slow us down, remind us that before we jump to the solution, we need to see all the parts. We'll talk all about integration of our own emotion in the third section of this book. But for now, our primary power comes in this place of simply acknowledging another as a key to not only changing lives but saving them. It's a task that becomes one we can take on, even on our most tired days.

We put a huge emphasis on regulated emotion in the people we love, or we serve, or we lead. Again, we love it when people are calm. It's predictable, and it's safe. You'll remember that emotional dysregulation involves three things: uncertainty, fear, and no end in sight. See, there's an unpredictability to being dysregulated. As humans, we prefer, generally speaking, to know what to expect. We want to know what comes next. Now, some of us are bigger planners than others, but the deal for many of us is that our body is much more inclined to relax when we know what's in store. Hence, there's a huge desire to jump to the fix or the answer when people we love are distressed.

As a psychologist, I've spent a lot of time talking about strategies to help a kid or a big person deal with something that is troubling them. Maybe it's an intrusive memory, maybe it's a behavior, maybe it's a feeling like anxiety or depression. Often it's the actions of another person that we would just like to (significantly) alter. When we evoke strategies without understanding what we are fixing or how the symptom or the problem got there, we often miss the mark. In his groundbreaking book based on his trauma research, Bruce Perry (along with contributions by Oprah Winfrey)[1] writes about the importance of shifting the question from "What's wrong with you?" to "What happened to you?" When somebody is inappropriate or unkind, or tells you to fuck off because "you're fat and dumb," it's difficult not to focus on that behavior. It often, so easily, becomes personal and dysregulating. But does it change anything when you know what happened to put that person in that place of responding in that particular way? Again, let me be clear. It's not that we condone or forgive or allow that to happen. It's much more about taking back the power. You become so much more powerful when you know how to acknowledge first. Because you stay regulated.

One of the most remarkable things about acknowledgment that gets me every time I watch it in action is that when an emotion is identified and seen, it calms. Even a simple acknowledgment matters; however, we have a collective refusal to acknowledge the things that hurt us. We always have. For example, the one thing we can be sure of is that we are all, eventually, going to die. But we don't like to talk about it. We don't like to plan for it or even acknowledge the possibility. In Canada, for instance, according to an Angus Reid Institute poll, half of people over the age of 55 don't have a will.[2] In the only thing we know for sure, at least half of us will avoid even talking about, let alone planning for, the inevitable. We're not a fan of the hard emotions. Given the chance, we'll avoid them and just hope they will pass us by or fade away. See, there's a universal need, regardless of the concerning human issue we face, to avoid the dysregulation and move to the "We're good? We're good!" part of our relationships, marriages, and organizations, and even our children's well-being. We just want it to all be okay.

Experiences of trauma, and perhaps most notably the reckoning with the cultural genocide that Canada is facing, is the truest example of that. We've attempted, for years, to move into the reconciliation phase of the Truth and Reconciliation Commission's Final Report regarding our Indigenous Peoples, before truly understanding or fully acknowledging the atrocities that occurred. As we outlined in the trauma chapter, the cultural genocide of Indigenous Peoples in North America has always been known, but rarely taught or talked about outside of Indigenous communities. Why? In part, there is so much pain, embarrassment, maybe the fear of repercussions, that the desire to "just move on" becomes palpable.

OUR CALL TO ACTION

The word "acknowledgment" has become particularly sexy. I've heard it now more than ever, particularly as we attempt to reconcile the multiple generations of unacknowledged hurt in Canada. In fact, the deepest understanding of this word "acknowledgment" for me has come from the incredible Indigenous Peoples who have been gracious enough to teach me. As we outlined briefly, the cultural genocide of Indigenous Peoples in North America is a story that is not history; it continues to unfold. Unmarked graves at the sites of residential school sites are still being unearthed, and our foster care system within North America is dramatically, disproportionately serving Indigenous children.[3] These facts serve as testament to the multiple generations of trauma inflicted on peoples that left many unable to care for their next generations because of their own, often debilitating, trauma. Across many marginalized communities, the call for acknowledgment (and of course reparative and reformative action) is imperative.

In fact, land acknowledgments have been a practice in place for hundreds of years before the arrival of the colonizers. When Indigenous peoples visited other territories, it was, and still is, customary to respect and acknowledge the traditional custodians of the land. Recent versions of land acknowledgments, spoken by non-Indigenous people, have been inspired by the 94 calls to action published in the Truth and Reconciliation Commision's Final Report. Within that report, it was asked of Indigenous Peoples, "What do you need as we begin to assess, address, and heal?" A primary request was for acknowledgment. Today, doing a land acknowledgment can serve as a single act of reconciliation.

Now, reading a land acknowledgment is easy to do from a performative perspective. I have identified on websites and in documents the land on which I "work, live, and play," but so many times I did this because someone told me I should. Further, having spoken across North America over the past five years, I will tell you that I have, embarrassingly so, "sat through" many land acknowledgments without truly understanding the gravity of the words. I have heard many people comment and have been a part of conversations where the response (often accompanied by an eye roll) includes something like "How many times do we have to do this?" or "Is it ever going to be enough?" or "We said it yesterday," or worse yet, "Let's move on." Another popular phrase I've heard thrown around at speeches and holiday dinners includes something like "We've already apologized; (insert any formal government or religious official's name here) issued a formal apology already. What more do they want?" And so often, I've heard the names of the lands to be acknowledged phonetically butchered because the time wasn't taken to learn the correct pronunciation.

As I become more and more aware of my own deeply embedded racial biases (some of which we just started to explore in the previous section), a few things about acknowledgments have become starkly clear to me. First, for an acknowledgment to be most effective, there are two things it isn't and one thing it must be.

WHAT IT ISN'T

First, a true acknowledgment isn't an apology. We are often sorry for people's pain. "Sorry for your loss" is a common, sometimes empty phrase that we insert when we don't know what else to say. Don't get me wrong, apologies are critical when we are attempting to repair or address someone else's hurt, but an acknowledgment, to me, is something so much deeper and more powerful.

It's a "bearing witness to" before ever inserting your own feelings on another. There is no desire, necessarily, in an acknowledgment to fix anything (just yet). Although action is necessary, we want to jump there too quickly. With respect to Indigenous Peoples, for example, just think of how ludicrous this would sound: "Sorry for the cultural genocide. We good?" There is, of course, the desperate attempt to make it right, especially when the pain inflicted has been great. I get it—this part makes sense to me—there is the desire to get back to where all is calm and all is bright, to unload shame even. But so often in that process of apologies, there's the assumption that the "sin is forgiven" and, so again, an acknowledgment is not about apologizing.

The second thing an acknowledgment isn't is a one-shot deal. "Will it ever be enough?" we ask. "Isn't it time to move on already?" In a powerful response to the question, "Why can't you get over it?" Indigenous leader, lawyer, and former Canadian senator, the Honorable Murray Sinclair, asks, "Why can't you remember it?" See, when it comes to mitigating the effects of a cultural genocide, the question "Will anyone ever be able to acknowledge it 'enough?'" has a very clear answer: "No." In our lifetimes, the healing power of genuine acknowledgment will never be enough, for a salve cannot instantly heal a tender, still-festering wound. The simple desire to be seen, for all of us, even when there isn't a massive, gaping hole, is biologically necessary. We are wired for connection. I often hear similar sentiments in all kinds of relationship contexts in my office. Things like, "All I do is give"; or "Will it ever be enough for her?" Another common sentiment: "I tried that relationship thing, and it didn't work." Again, when we're talking about relationships that are important to us, you and I, as humans, function best when we are connected. The one thing that ties us all together is a deep desire to know we matter. To be seen.

The healthiest among us are very clear that even in the most secure situations, in the most confident and competent of beings, we will always need connection, reassurance, a regulating other. When people, particularly when they matter to us, stop to look and truly see us—and most especially when they don't look away when it gets messy—that's when so much strength is garnered. And at our best, we know that people around us are willing to bear witness to our personal experiences and truths.

Acknowledging our fellow humans, in most any capacity, is quite simply magic. I mean it. Just imagine, if you're a parent, for example, how you would respond if you're out frolicking in your community tomorrow and someone comes up to you and says, "Hey (they call you specifically by your name)/I just wanted to tell you, I think your daughter is amazing. I don't know what you're doing but you're doing something right. She's always so kind to my kid. I just wanted you to know." What happens to you if you are the parent of that child who somebody just acknowledged as amazing? I'll tell you what you do first, before you get too excited: You confirm they're talking about your child. You don't want to have them say, "Oh shit, sorry. I thought you were somebody else." So, you often take this middle step of clarifying your child's name, and once that part has been confirmed, then a few very predictable things happen. First, we get closer physically—we lean in. Second, our voice rises a few octaves, and we say things like "Ahh! Thank you so much." And then after, we feel very connected and committed to returning that feeling, and so sometimes we say things like "I love your coat"; or suddenly you find yourself inviting the acknowledger over for wine. We're so inclined to return acknowledgments because they regulate us. We love that feeling so much. But if we're not too stunned or suspicious, we find ourselves in a place to return that experience. Do you see? It's contagious.

WHAT IT MUST BE

In recent months as I have talked about what an acknowledgment isn't, it has occurred to me that it also must be one thing—genuine. So many people said, particularly in the pandemic fog, that they were tired of hearing the generic responses of "thank you for your service" or "we'll get through this together." The blanket email from "the top" wasn't encouraging in any way; in fact, it felt condescending and maddening. The need for a genuine, authentic connection is so much more powerful. Consider this for a second: You walk outside of your workplace; it's late and you're exhausted. You still have so much to do tonight at home. You've missed dinner (again). You've been working your ass off. And as you sink into the driver's seat, you notice a note tucked under your windshield wiper. Reluctantly and with a long sigh, you get out of your car and pull out the note. And there, in handwritten prose, are words intended just for you. It starts with your name. And it's followed by words like these: "I just wanted you to know that I am inspired by you. I watch how hard you work. Thank you for showing us the way. I hope you have a good night and get to relax because if anyone deserves it, it's you."

Just imagine what would happen to you when you read those words? Now, in all honesty, it depends on who it's from and whether you can sink into it or not. But I promise you, more times than not what happens is we'll look around to make sure nobody's around and then we might start to cry. At the very least, we shake our heads or drop our shoulders. Could it be true that someone has noticed? There is a neurochemical response, even if we can't feel it. See, sometimes we spend so much of our energy in a heightened state of arousal, where anger is much more accessible. Anger, even exhaustion, is an easy defense. And what happens when somebody acknowledges you specifically? They're not apologizing. It's not a generic, superficial nod; it's genuine, and the anger starts to dissipate, even if only for a few moments.

It reminds me of this story I told in *Kids These Days* about a patient I had early in my career, a patient I wish I could have back. This kid was 12 and she was so mad. For the first two weeks of her admission, there were multiple calls for security. I had been kicked and hit and scratched as I tried to sit with her to figure out what was "wrong" with her. She rarely spoke to me. She was "non-compliant" and refused to participate in sessions. In her whole six-week admission, I can remember her saying only one real sentence. After we had endured a particularly long meltdown, she was exhausted and, sadly, so was I. I sat down on the floor of the secure room, looked at her, and desperately pleaded, "What am I missing?" She looked me directly in the eye (the first and last time she looked at me during that admission) and said, "Don't you know that mad is just sad's bodyguard?"

Whew. Even now, it takes my breath away. I will never forget that moment. Back then, I was too focused on fixing her. I didn't understand what the hell she meant. And now, years later, that kid taught me one of the most important lessons she knew I needed to learn in my career: It's not what's wrong with you; it is so truly and genuinely what happened to you. Since that moment, I have never met a "mad" who wasn't sad. Underneath every mad is an authentic raw feeling that is sometimes so protected (always for good reason) it becomes difficult to get to. See, mad is often the cover for not just sad, but often a host of other equally debilitating, more specific emotions like fear, hurt, shame, helplessness, humiliation, jealousy, outrage at injustice, embarrassment, or rejection. This doesn't mean anger, as an emotion, isn't important or necessary. It is indeed both these things. But it can often be so distracting or inappropriate that it acts as a mask for the emotion closest to the soul. Anger, in my experience, never has contact with the purest, most vulnerable parts of us. There's always a buffer emotion (or two or three or four) layered in there.

Part of the way through that hard exterior of anger is acknowledgment. If I could have her back today, I would have said "tell me more." There would have been a lot more snacks and informal visits. I would have also spent more time understanding the things, people, and places she loved the most. Because all I saw was a kid who got kicked out of school, ran away from home, dressed in dark clothes, and was so "mean, attention-seeking, and manipulative" to so many people who were just trying to "help." Sadly, I learned years later something that I had missed: There had been significant abuse happening within the home. Her parents, at the time, presented as connected and loving, albeit significantly overwhelmed. I didn't spend enough time asking them about their stories, their shame, their guilt. See, when we can hold space for the big emotions, that's what matters to sad.

As a settler, I am now just beginning to understand the importance of acknowledgments so much more deeply, primarily because of the teachings of Indigenous Peoples. So, I would like to acknowledge, as I did at the beginning of this book but even more importantly now, the land where I'm sitting, writing to you:

All the things on these pages were primarily created on Treaty 7 land here in what is also called Alberta, Canada. It is home of the traditional and ancestral territory of the Blackfoot Confederacy, made up of the Kainai, Piikani and Siksika as well as the Tsuut'ina Nation and Stoney Nakoda First Nation and the Métis Nation Region Three.

Every day I become more and more aware of the honor and privilege it is to learn and unlearn here. One of the many asks is to never forget how we, particularly as white settlers, got here. I never, not one time, had to worry about having my children taken away to an institution, shrouded as a "school." Never have I had to consider if the water I was drinking was clean or how food was able to grow so easily on the lands where I grew up. My promise is to show my children how to be better. To acknowledge first means to listen and take direction on how to assist in the healing. If we ask for direction and don't listen to the response, we have missed, well, everything.

When I had the honor to sit in the presence of Chief Cadmus Delorme, a Cree and Saulteaux man who is a citizen and currently Chief of the Cowessess First Nation, he reminded me that the ask is not for guilt or shame for the years of cultural genocide that is the history of Canada. As he so beautifully explained, our job in moving forward is to teach our children to be better and to do better. The ask from Indigenous Peoples is also that we listen and understand and acknowledge the truth before we ever consider reconciliation. That is what you and I, if you're so inclined, can continue to do. Acknowledge, hold space, have empathy for, seek to understand, and then relentlessly take that direction, raise voices, and act. Then do that again, for the rest of our days.

PUTTING YOUR MONEY WHERE YOUR MOUTH IS

Now, I want to be clear that an acknowledgment is the first step. Action must always follow—but action is often so empty if the acknowledgment doesn't happen first. You don't know what to treat if you don't first assess where the pain originated. And then when they tell you it's a broken leg, you don't start fixing the arm because you think you know better. You can't get to the reconciliation part before landing in the truth. I think often about the parallels between emotional regulation and attending to behavior. It is a two-step process. It's not enough just to calm someone and never teach. It's also never enough to simply acknowledge and not act. You can't teach a flipped lid. Similarly, when you act without acknowledgment, you often miss the thing that so many humans need first, before they're able to appreciate the act: to be seen.

What does action look like? Raise voices, advocate for, buy from. That is the key. You can't tell anyone that you're doing the work to be kind and empathic, that you are committed to inclusivity or anti-racist work. You must show them. Although words are critical as the necessary first step, if they're not followed by actions, the sincerity of acknowledgment becomes questioned, particularly when no one is watching. There isn't one of us who is good enough to undo systemic oppression. Not a senior leader, a president, a prime minister, a CEO, or a priest. Collectively, it is up to you and me, every single day, doing the next, best, right, kind thing. The time is now, dear ones. I've never been surer of that.

BRINGING IT BACK HOME

Acknowledgment is the necessary ointment that we so often miss. It is clear that it isn't either of two things—an apology or a one-shot deal. Maybe most importantly, it must be genuine. This act of holding space, of appreciating, is absolutely the key to so many things, including strong relationships and successful teams. It can feel like we're not doing anything—which probably means you're doing it right. It can feel helpless to just listen. To get out of our own heads where our own judgment, guilt, and pain live to make room for the experience of another. This understanding will lead us beautifully into the next chapter all about empathy. Because now that we have some rules around what an acknowledgment is and isn't, the question becomes, how do we get good at it? Over the next few chapters I want to unpack a few things I think are critical to getting good at the acknowledging power we all have, and so rarely use:

1. Consider the last time someone genuinely acknow-ledged you. What did you notice the most about that experience? How did it leave you feeling?
2. What sacred territory are you currently living on?
3. Watch what happens the next time you hand out a genuine compliment. Just notice how it is received (or rejected). And, what it feels like to give it (regardless of the response).

CHAPTER EIGHT

Empathy

THE BEST PLAYER ON THE POWER PLAY

I f I had to choose one skill I could keep if I had to give up all the rest, it would be empathy. If I could have one hope for the world, I would wish that we would all get remarkably well-practiced at that skill. I think some of our most important work is about our capacity to seek first to understand before being understood. And I don't think we spend nearly enough time talking about it. The kicker is that empathy is a skill. You're not born with it. And just like any other skill, it takes practice. Truly being able to suspend judgment and imagine what another person feels is a damn gift. And it's the one thing some of the best in this business of life get good at.

In a recent meta-analysis of 146 different definitions of empathy, researchers suggested it's best defined as "the ability to experience affective and cognitive states of another person, while maintaining a distinct self, in order to understand the other."[1] And maybe the most powerful string of words that helped me truly understand this emotion: "Empathy is a tool of compassion. We can respond empathically only if we're willing to be present to someone's pain. If we're not willing to do that, it's not real empathy."[2] One of the further caveats is the necessity to temporarily put aside how we experience a situation to allow ourselves to feel another person's truth. Herein lies the critical part about empathy: It needs us to temporarily suspend judgment. Empathy means listening to seek an understanding if, and especially *when*, you don't agree with or condone what is being said—or when you truly believe that the other person's truth is outrageous or even blatantly wrong.

IT'S NOT A LOT OF THINGS

Empathy is not sympathy—which is how we feel toward another person and can sound like "I'm sorry *for* you." We often mistake these two. Sympathy can sometimes be experienced as pity; in fact, it has been said that empathy and pity are first cousins,[3] but they're portrayed and experienced entirely differently. Empathy is soft and inviting, while pity is hard and demeaning. Further, empathy is not projection, which happens when we say things like "I know exactly what that's like. I lost my mother, too." In projection, the shift in focus is from them to us. Projection's often a well-meaning attempt to align ourselves with another who we think may know our depths of pain. However, it often comes at the expense of disregarding another's experience because it's rarely (if ever) exactly like yours. Empathy is also not reflection—which many of us counseling types are taught and is quite frankly one of the more disconnecting things you can do. A simple reflection might sound like "I see you're feeling sad." Or, "You appear to be feeling anger." Even as I type those words, I want to throat punch whoever is saying them to me. There's no connection in a mere reflection. Empathy is also not about becoming overwhelmed by the other person's experience. We remain rooted in ourselves but seek to understand another's view of the world as they experience it; to attempt deeply and truly to understand what another is feeling about an experience.

This part is the most important when we talk about empathy—and often where many of us jump off the empathy train because it's that most difficult caveat to wrap our heads around: True empathy doesn't require you to even agree with or accept another person's position. Empathy happens in the spaces before judgment. It happens when you're just trying to "get it," not decide if it's right or wrong, or if it even makes sense. That's particularly why it's so difficult to not just jump past it.

I see this so often when I work with families, usually with a teenager in the mix. Parents who are trying to have empathy for their struggling adolescent, who maybe wants to sneak out of the house or try marijuana or go away for the weekend with their boyfriend/girlfriend at 15. It becomes difficult to practice empathy, to temporarily suspend judgment, and to try to deeply and truly understand what another might be feeling when we're scared for their safety, or when we know they just don't get it. It can sometimes feel, when we take an empathic approach, that we can somehow unwittingly get sucked into supporting our teenager's decision, and we miss the opportunity to teach a lesson. Empathy, however, is not about the "what you do next" part. Empathy doesn't dictate how you decide, as a parent, or a partner, or a manager what it is you *do* with the information. That is the next step. Empathy is just that sacred space of seeking to understand it first. It is the quintessential "how" that is embedded in the most powerful acts of acknowledgment. The biggest caveat I think I've learned about empathy is this: By holding space for truly understanding what somebody else might be feeling, where they might be coming from, or the perspective they're landing in, it doesn't mean you will necessarily support, believe, or condone it.

YOU KNOW WHEN YOU GET IT RIGHT

There's no single way of communicating empathy—it's kind of an all-in, verbal, and nonverbal attempt at knowing. The more empathy becomes a genuine full-body experience for you, the giver of empathy, the more powerfully it tends to be received. It's about creating a shared understanding so that there's no longer a feeling of being alone in an experience. The most genuine moments of empathy often require vulnerable and sometimes raw access to the soul. If we want to get technical, however, researchers have identified four main attributes of empathy.[4; 5; 6]

The first is perspective-taking, which is identified as the ability to take someone else's perspective and recognize it as truth, even if you have not had similar experiences (e.g., you don't have to be a foster kid to imagine what it might be like). The second is avoiding judgments. Judgments cloud clarity (obviously); however, temporarily putting aside your own thoughts and feelings, as we outlined above, is truly the greatest test that empathy presents. Turns out, the more strongly you disagree with the person you're attempting to empathize with, the more difficult this is to do (and it's often when it's needed the most). Third is recognizing emotion in another person. And this, of course, requires some skill in dual awareness—having the ability to get out of your own head and slow down long enough to notice in another person, by way of body language, eye contact, or tone of voice, that what they might be thinking is unique to them and possibly different from what you are thinking, in turn. Empathy's final attribute is the ability to communicate an understanding of the other's lived experience, either verbally or nonverbally. This is where it's handy to have a few words in the emotional language tank. But even if you don't have them, empathy is often communicated best with no words. An exercise in grad school really brought it home for me. The instructions are simply to find someone who would be willing to tell you, in two minutes' time, about a minor problem they're experiencing. As they do it the first time, your only job is to seem as uninterested as possible via your body language and your words. You can communicate, but the one rule is you can't ask any questions. At the end of the two minutes, ask how it felt. Then, do it one more time, getting the person to explain the problem for two minutes. This time, again without questions, be as genuinely engaged and interested as you're able, particularly with your body language (sit facing the person, make eye contact, and keep your tone soft). At the end of the two minutes, once again ask how it felt. And equally as important, notice how both those experiences felt for you. One of the cool things about empathy for me is you know when you land it. The recipient will communicate it clearly, and you will feel it, too.

Conversely, the opposite is also true. You can feel it, plain as day, when someone doesn't get it. For example, I tried to understand what it might have felt like for a patient I'd been seeing for two years to come to terms with an affair that had been happening for six of the seven years of her marriage. I tried on words like "betrayed" or "abandoned," and I could tell they didn't quite fit. Turns out, it wasn't the betrayal that was the hardest part—it was that she felt so incompetent for not trusting her intuition. She said, "I just feel so 'stupid.'" Suddenly, it all made sense. The pieces fit together even better when we linked feeling "stupid" to experiences with her father in which she was belittled for not being as smart as her siblings. How could she have missed it? That was fodder for many rich discussions around just how much she could trust herself and how smart she was when it came to knowing what she needed. She wasn't "stupid," after all. That shifted a number of things for her in the relationships she would build (and potentially rebuild) moving forward. I could see her physically look lighter. It reminded me, once again, that each of us has our own truths. Just witnessing this in another is such a critical piece.

And here's the cool thing. It seems that when you can use language to unlock an unidentified feeling, it's often the gateway to more layers or insights or understandings. The closer you get to the self—that core we talked about in the first part of this book—the rawer and purer the emotions become. This component of acknowledgment feels like another piece of cultivating meaningful connection. It's practicing the courage to walk alongside and resisting telling another how they feel or how they might have got there—all of which aligns nicely with the importance of simply acknowledging.

WE THINK WE'RE GOOD AT IT. WE'RE NOT.

Humans are social beings, and everyone has the capacity to develop empathy; however, you're not born with empathy. You must receive it first and experience it in order to have the ability to give it away. And like any skill you want to hone—like your golf swing, yoga, or spirituality—it's a practice.

In training therapists and supervising promising clinicians, I am often amazed at how difficult it is for so many of us to truly imagine the experience of another person. In theory, we think we're really good at it. But again, the desire to "fix it," or say the right thing, often impedes us from truly feeling with another in their experience because so often we're stuck in our own heads. I clearly remember the shifts as I grew as a clinician when I had moments of realizing that I didn't have to have the answer to the next step at every juncture—often because it was never what the client needed. In fact, when I truly wanted to understand what the other was experiencing, whether I agreed, condoned, supported it or not, and just allowed myself to trust the process, it felt like freedom. We often want, so desperately, to help or to offer the thing that will relieve the tension or the pain, especially if we love the person or are the one in charge of making them "better." The answer always seems to come back to the necessary step of seeking to genuinely understand the experience of another. To give them the gift of feeling seen.

See, we all have only one reference point when we're trying to make sense of someone else's story. And it's entirely innate (and normal) to compare ourselves to others, even when we're making an effort to have a genuine, selfless empathic experience with another. The heart of comparison stems from our struggles with our own worthiness. A clear access to your ability for empathy is paved when you do your own "work." (We'll talk more about what that really means—coming up).

COMPARATIVE SUFFERING

This leads so beautifully into the idea of comparative suffering. Theodore Roosevelt said that comparison is the thief of all joy. And there are many intricacies in this complex phenomenon. My favorite definition of comparison may be its ultimate message: It's the desire to "simultaneously fit in and stand out." Indeed, it's the unattainable quest to be like everyone else, but better.[7] Comparative suffering happens when someone tries to make sense of their own pain by comparing it to someone else's. We all do this to a certain extent; it's beneficial when it provides perspective. The danger, however, is that it minimizes the legitimacy of our feelings, and it may impede our ability to stay with the feelings of another. Comparative suffering can end in two damaging outcomes. Either it may leave you feeling like people with "smaller" suffering aren't worth the effort; or, conversely, it may make you feel like your own suffering isn't significant. Both feelings can be debilitating.

Sometimes people don't talk because of the shame. Sometimes people don't tell their stories because they think others won't believe them. And I think what strikes me is that often people don't talk or tell the stories of their trauma because they don't want to hurt the people they love. They don't want the people they love to experience it, too. Or sometimes we fear that if we really tell people how we're feeling, they'll look at us differently, knowing what we've endured or how we sometimes think. We've even heard our parents or grandparents saying, "You have no idea how difficult it was in our generation. Consider yourself lucky. We had to walk to school uphill both ways. You don't know how good you have it." Although the intention is to assist in our being grateful, sometimes it stifles the next generation into considering that their experience can't compare and so may be unworthy of acknowledgment.

I've seen this so many times in couples who have a beautiful love story hidden underneath all the desperation just to be seen. "You think you have it bad! I'm the one who looks after the kids, gets the groceries, and works full time." What becomes so critical in this process, as we've discussed frequently, is the ability to identify the words to feel with another person. And furthermore, I often think what fucks us up the most in this comparison game is that we become divisive in the way we categorize each other and ultimately ourselves. We say things like "She's a much better mom than me"; or, "He went through all that trauma, I didn't." These pedestals or pits we put others (and ourselves) on or in leave very little room for gray in this comparison game. See, I think there's often a very short walk between our internal understanding of "I'm great" and "I'm a useless piece of shit."

EMOTIONS ARE TAUGHT DIFFERENTLY
TO THOSE WHO HAVE A PENIS

Sometimes people don't talk because they don't have the words to say the things. Sometimes it's because they weren't taught the words. I think this is particularly common among men (or those who identify with a masculine energy) largely because, for a litany of reasons, women are better at the emotional language game.[8] In so many of the important shifts necessary to reconnect us in this disconnected world, I think those who identify as female will, and must be, at the helm. I am aware of how binary that statement is. As a mother of two sons and the wife of a (fairly) phenomenal husband, I promise you this: men, women, and the spectrum in between are all profoundly important. Obviously, there are distinct biological differences in the anatomy and physiology. What isn't different, however, are the emotions that we, as humans, are made up of. Now more than ever, we need those of us who are better equipped with an emotional language to step up and step out in positions of leadership and mentorship, primarily because, once again, we can't tell them—we must show them. We (I'm speaking as someone who identifies as a woman) have to really know we require a seat at the table because we have so much of what the world needs. I wonder, in fact, if it's wise to consider it the *responsibility* of those of us with an emotional language to lead the way back home—to a connected, feeling understood way of operating.

BETTER, BUT NOT FAST ENOUGH

We like to think we are now so much better at gender equity. Perhaps understanding gender identity is progressing, I'm willing to give in there, but I think we have a long way to go. Think about the last time you walked into a toy store—one of those big box–store types. At this very moment, around the globe, these stores are clearly set up in a divisive way—blue and pink. A penis section and a vagina section respectively. What's most available in the penis section? Guns, trucks, tractors, hockey sticks, baseball bats. The tough, rough and tumble stuff. Look across the aisle to the vagina section. The colors change, the softness appears. There are dolls and food and things to be nurtured. From a very early age (read: conception) we speak to, interact with, and move very differently through the world, depending on whether we bring a "son" or a "daughter" home from the hospital. Our families respond differently. We hold the child differently. We speak to the child differently. Listen, even before our babies take their first breath, we are creating stories. Now that technological advances have allowed for the ever-popular gender-reveal parties, think about what happens when anticipating parents shoot pink confetti out of a rocket or you bite into the cake and it's pink. Typically, the octaves go higher and there's a softening of the crowd, a leaning in, as we consider what it will be like to raise a daughter. If the confetti tube shoots blue, there tends to be more chest bumping; cue the talking hockey or football, and maybe even a crush of the odd beer can on a forehead. These often-occurring stereotypical responses don't happen because we're bad people, but there are significantly entrenched gender norms that center largely on antiquated roles of "suck it up" and "be tough" kind of power versus "soft and gentle" submissiveness with a side of "nurturing and patience."

As a minor hockey coach, I hear this almost weekly: "You're playing like a bunch of girls." Or, "Suck it up. Boys don't cry." The intent here is often beautiful—I want you to be okay. I want you to not make a big deal about it. I want you to toughen up. I don't want you to hurt and be unable to handle the hard emotions in the world. We tend to do this more vehemently with the children we parent or are the most connected to. Typically, when we have less investment (like, let's say you're talking to your best friend's kid), we have more room to wonder about emotions and make space for the hard things. The more responsibility we feel for the well-being of a particular child, the more inclined we are to get them back sooner to "calm." And regardless of the relationship, most of us have far less tolerance for a boy's emotions that we do for a girl's.[9]

This discrepancy is perhaps most clear with stereotypical teen-age girls. Often, we hear people describe this cohort as emotional or dramatic, often in comparison to aloof, less emotional, teenage boys. This dichotomy often makes me mad. We have given girls the emotional language to describe the shit-show of emotion that happens in their bodies during adolescence, and for the most part, it's remarkably helpful when they're "emotional and dramatic" because we made them that way. The job of a teenager is to try out the rush of emotions and experiences in a body that so often is not ready for any of it. They're thrust into a social context of others who also are not ready for it. These not-ready-for-its spend a lot of time together, spinning in isolation because they think they can handle it all. This, of course, is where big people come in. Not to stifle or punish, but ideally (as often as possible, anyway) to give those huge, often messy, sometimes ridiculous emotions, some space.

Recently, I had the mom of a family I'd been working with call in distress. She explained that her 12-year-old daughter had talked to her the night before about all the thoughts running through her head. She'd thought about cutting and felt like she was "depressed." This mama was demanding I see her daughter immediately. I did my best to collect this mom first, and then I reminded her that, in her beautiful efforts to give her daughter an emotional language, she created this. Mom, unimpressed, suggested that it might have been easier if her sweet daughter didn't "have all these words."

Then where would all these emotions go? Together, we agreed, our only job was to give her daughter a place to put them, first. And then guide her accordingly. Further to this, I always find it interesting that our often very "emotional" female-identifying humans then sometimes marry those sometimes "unemotional" male-identifying humans. They get into marriages and say things like "He never talks about anything. I have no idea how he's feeling." Right? If there's no emotional language there, it'll be very difficult to give it away. How do we create safe spaces for our boys, our sons, our partners (anybody on this human spectrum, really), to be able to explore what it means to feel? As a mom, my hope for kids these days, particularly my own, is that they're not simply "happy," but that they will feel deeply and truly all the emotions that we experience in this world, and always have somewhere to put them.

LEADING THE WAY

Can those who don't have an emotional language get one? Hell, yes. Again, it happens so much more frequently in the showing and not the telling. Coming to terms with our own expectations and biases as we interact with our children—or the ones we coach or teach or care for—means acknowledging our own tendency to slip into stereotypes and expectations. What makes me know that this is so dire now more than ever is that all of us, but our boys (or those who identify as such) in particular, need a place to put emotions. Anxiety, depression, all the big ones won't kill you—they simply can't. But, again, not talking about them might.

Those "corrective experiences" of being seen by another can happen throughout our lifetimes and effectively change the way we see the world and allow ourselves to feel seen within it. Often, these corrective experiences happen for our kids within the education system, on well-coached teams, or when leadership teams are led by someone who is adamant that kindness and relationship must come first before the intolerance of bullshit. I am blown away by the ingenuity of programs designed specifically for those who identify as boys, like the WiseGuyz program developed for Grade 9 boys to promote healthy relationships and prevent adolescent dating violence. It's designed to address, head on, the impacts of harmful gender stereotypes. And further, a Canadian nonprofit called Next Gen Men, whose programs are designed to change how the world sees, acts, and thinks about masculinity, has incredible resources for schools and communities. We're starting to shift the narrative, friends, and I'm here for all of it. Further, and even more accessibly, is just the slowing down, on-purpose connections that we all have the capacity to make with each other, right here, in this moment. I have a few tried and true tricks that I'll leave for you right here just in case you need 'em.

EMPATHY DRILLS

For any skill-building game, there are often strategies and suggestions to be able to play the game better—and empathy is no exception. Although many have written extensively about what it takes to engage completely in a relationship with another, I want to include the top four strategies I often share when giving a talk. They're foolproof ways that seem to have a magic power of putting others at ease. From a neurological perspective, each of them, to varying degrees, does the job of pulling the prefrontal cortex back on. You might also notice that the more genuinely you engage in each of these strategies, the more effective they become. Although not an exhaustive list, these are my go-tos when talking to leaders, coaches, parents, and partners, and I hope you can use them, too.

THE LIGHT-UP

I like to think of the "light-up" as the starting lineup of any empathic experience. I talked a lot about this concept in *Kids These Days*. You know that feeling when you haven't seen a kid you love in a long time and then you lay eyes on them, and they run to you with open arms and you just lose your mind with joy? Think airport reunions or those videos on TikTok where military members come back from deployment and surprise their partners or their moms. (I can spend hours sobbing while watching these.) That rush of emotion you can see in their faces and feel in their response to each other—that is the epitome of the light-up. And it's all we need. We never grow out of wanting the people we love to lose their minds, or to light up when they see us. We're so much better at lighting up in relationships when we feel a reciprocal connection—those are the ones where we tend to look and see the most.

Overall, this might be one of my favorite strategies because you can unbelievably impact your community today, in this moment, by simply waving like you're the most excited you've ever been at every stop sign or stop light the next time you drive anywhere. You basically become an instant mobile mental health unit in your little corner of the world. Yesterday, an older feller out for his morning walk almost threw his neck out trying to figure out what the hell all the waving was about when I got his attention with an emphatic wave as I drove by. I love seeing how surprised people are. My kids and I even count how many people we can get to wave back at us on the school drop-off drives in the morning (beats fighting over whose turn it is to sit in the front or which one of them forgot their agendas). Just notice the responses you get. So often, it does just as much for you as it does for them.

FACE TO FACE

The second empathy drill I think is helpful to practice is simply eye contact. The whole concept of not just looking but seeing what others experience and how we, as a human race, are far more alike than we are different often starts with the slowing down and looking. This specific strategy—face to face—is meant to remind us that the physical act of meeting the eyes of another, assuming they're physically and culturally able to do so, is powerful and so often left unused. Consider this: Where are your eyes when you are anxious or depressed? Where were your eyes the last time you were the saddest you've ever been? Where are your eyes when you're not doing well in relationships with people you love? You avoid people at all costs. I'll tell you, with my own personal husband, if we're having a knockdown, shoot 'em out disagreement about something and we're in our galley kitchen, I become a master at exploring the pots and pans drawer. Conversely, where are your eyes when you are confidently explaining the things you love? Or when you're trying to discover if a child you love is injured or sick? You do your best to get their eyes.

Ironically, to be able to look into the eyes of the people you love will remain the hardest thing you will ever do. Although I get it, I hate this truth. The more you mean to me—like if I spend a lot of time with you at home or even at work—the progressively harder it becomes to sit face to face with you. "The eyes are the window to your soul," Shakespeare (and others) wrote. The opportunities we take not only to look at each other but to truly see, however, are becoming more and more limited.

We have never had so many juicy opportunities to look elsewhere. The allure of social media and Netflix makes a distraction far easier than having a potentially difficult conversation with the people we love. Turns out, there are no opportunities for rejection when I'm watching someone else's life unfold on-screen. Yet the more we do this, the less able we become at having any conversation at all and we're left feeling even more disconnected. Again, it's a thing you have to practice if you want to get good at it. And the less we do it, the less able we're going to be at giving away.

There's a body of research I love, which originated with psychologist Arthur Aron, that beautifully highlights this face-to-face empathy builder.[10] The task is simple. Ask somebody you love, like a partner, your sibling, a parent, or one of your grown children, to sit with you and simply look at you for four minutes. I'm smiling when I write this because when I ask the group of people in a room where I'm speaking to do this with their partner that night, there's often a lot of laughter and a lot of eye rolling. I hear things like "Four minutes is so long!" "Look at him for four minutes to connect? It didn't even take four minutes for us to make the last baby" (true story).

I tried it with my husband. I said to him, "Honey, I was just reading this incredible research. Let's just sit on the couch right now, and I want us to just look at each other for four minutes." You know what he asked first? "Why?" I of course incredulously said, "because I'm your bride and we just should look at each other more." Now, here's the interesting thing about my husband. Imagine somebody the exact opposite of anything you know about me, and that would be Aaron. He's a scientist to the core. We have a spreadsheet for everything. Nothing is ever not planned to the excruciatingly painful last detail. And if there is the slightest possibility of a cost-saving measure, I promise you he will find it. The meticulousness is impressively annoying.

So, back to the story. We're sitting on the couch, he asks if I can set a timer for our four minutes of connection, and then he says, "Wait. Just stop for a second. Can I ask a question? What specifically am I looking for? Like did you get a haircut? Is this a new shirt?" (Seriously!) "Just let's look at each other!" I say. So, again, we initiate this process of the looking and he says, "Just one more question." (Sweet Jesus!) He says, after taking a deep breath, "Can we take breaks?" Are. You. Fuckin. Kidding. Me!? This task that I thought was going to be a simple, fun little foray into marital bliss has now turned into the need for a marital therapist. But I digress. We managed to make it four minutes and, in line with what Arthur Aron's research has shown, if you can make it through the first 30 seconds, there is typically a lot of giggling, laughter, being silly, checking the time. If you get into that first minute, you start to see things you haven't seen in a while. The caution here might be to consider not saying some of those things out loud, like "Holy shit, you're old." Or, "We really need to pluck your eyebrow hairs." Don't say those things.

Now, if you can manage to overcome those hurdles, you will arrive at this place at about the three-and-a-half-minute mark where you will start to feel something. Emotion? Is that you? Because here's the interesting thing about the people we love the most: So much of our stories happens in the spaces between words. As I sat there on the couch that day and looked at my husband, I remembered him sleeping on the floor of the Foothills Medical Centre for six days when our twin babies were born, and our son had to be in the neonatal intensive care unit. Aaron wouldn't leave my side. And I suddenly recalled what his face looked like on our wedding day. And I remembered that I've been on a journey with this man that no one else in this world knows about except the two of us. Not even our kids or our parents have seen the lines on his face like I have. It might be the most powerful thing that comes with reconnection. Not just looking, but finally seeing (or seeing anew) what's been there all along.

GET DOWN

The third little drill to add to your practice repertoire is a simple but highly effective add-on to the whole face-to-face thing: Get on the same level. There's a big difference when we look at each other and one is towering above versus sitting side by side. I've always maintained that some of the best conversations I've had with anyone— kids, my husband, my dad—happen in the car. Why? Because first, you're both seated in one of the only remaining socially acceptable small and confined spaces, and usually the door is locked and you're going at a high speed, which makes quick exits ill-advised. When we're on the same level as another human, we're more inclined to have our prefrontal cortex on than when we're not.

Even if we're not in a car, or in the same room, I want you to consider this drill because our days of online meetings and FaceTime interactions with the people we love will no doubt be a part of the rest of our lives. As you engage in online meetings or chats, ensure your camera is situated so that you're making direct eye contact—not like the FaceTime sessions I sometimes have with my parents, where I'm looking at a lot of nostrils. Or they forget they're on FaceTime and there's a close-up of the ear. Be sure a light is in front of you (the natural light from a window or an actual light), not behind you, so people can see your eyes. Although in-person interactions tend to be more powerful, often just hearing a familiar voice of someone we love can drop our cortisol levels and increase the feel-good chemicals in our brain like serotonin and dopamine. Physically spending time with people we love is truly a critically physiological experience.

FEED THEM AND THEY WILL COME (AROUND)

One of the most powerful strategies, and my personal favorite, comes down to snacks. Breaking out some sort of food as a regulating strategy is often a segue to an empathic conversation. From a behavioral perspective, we've long been taught to use food as a reward. For example, we do this frequently with our kids—we say things like, "You pee on the potty you get a Smartie." Or, you're allowed a "cheat meal" after you've put in all the work first. Here's the deal: You can't chew and swallow with a flipped lid—which means, if I get you chewing and swallowing, I can rest assured that I have access to the best parts of you. When we're most upset, particularly if we've engaged in a situation (or even a work shift) that is considered dysregulating, the last thing we want to do is eat. Sometimes it can be one of the most important things we can do—even if it's a sip of water or juice—so we can get back to a state of regulation. Many people have told me that when they're trying to "get through" to someone they love, especially when they can see them hurting, they will use words: "You have to talk to me." "What's wrong?" "What happened today?" As I'm sure you're aware, you can't make people talk. You can't get to the best parts of them (or you), including the ability for empathy, if the lid is flipped. So, offering a snack, having food at the ready when someone you love comes off shift or your babe needs that emergency fruit snack during a grocery store melt-down, can get us back to regulation, and thus access to our empathic ability, the quickest. The best acknowledgments of our shared commitment and love for each other often happens around a table full of food. And just for the record, although nutrition is important, pay attention to bringing all the snacks that will entice engagement. You can't regulate a kid with a carrot stick, right? And the last time you got your heart broken, the first stop (typically) wasn't a salad or an egg-white omelet. Food as a regulating strategy instead of as a reward was something many a grandmother knew to be true: Cook good food, and they will gather.

BRINGING IT BACK HOME

Empathy is your strongest player. It's a skill that takes time to get right, but it's perhaps the best use of your time to practice. Truly, genuinely feeling with another human is a very sacred space, where you're required to do nothing but simply be present. You can't do it when you're dysregulated, you don't want to do it when you're overwhelmed, and the people who need it the most are often the hardest to give it to. All these things add up to making this superpower so much easier said than done. It's much more than just being nice or reflecting back the emotions of another. Empathy for me, when done best, often has a spiritual feel. It's connecting on a level with a fellow human (someone you've known for years or a complete stranger) and feeling alongside them. It requires you to be open and, sometimes, even vulnerable, which is why we tend to avoid it. Most important for me, I think, is it's the single ingredient that makes the act of acknowledgment so powerful. Let's see if we can solidify this empathy thing just a little more:

1. Find someone, preferably a spouse if you have one or someone who means something to you, and try the four-minutes-of-connection experiment. It'll be so fun. And interesting for sure.
2. How often do you compare yourself to the experiences of others? Do you tend to search for those who have it "worse than me" or are you constantly looking at the ones who are "so much better than me"? There's no right answer here. It's just sometimes powerful to notice, as it often happens outside our awareness.

3. For the next three times you go for a drive, wave like you've just won the lottery at every stop light or stop sign. If you have passengers, don't tell them that's your plan, and see how they respond. And funner yet, catalog (in your mind) the responses you get back.

CHAPTER NINE

Be Kind and Don't Tolerate Bullshit
IN THAT ORDER

K indness is a real thing these days—suggestions on T-shirts, reminders on bumper stickers, and directives surrounding the importance of this act as the necessary gateway to all that is good. Kindness is a quality that involves being friendly, generous, or considerate. All words I like. It seems like it has become necessary to practice, on purpose, because the more disconnected we become, the less access we have to this ability that is synonymous with so many healing qualities.

Giving "it" away (i.e., time, resources, love) rather than having more and more for yourself brings about lasting well-being.[1] In fact, kindness has been found by researchers to be the most important predictor of satisfaction and stability in marriage.[2] Being kind to anyone, including a stranger, or even actively observing kindness around us, boosts happiness.[3] I was mildly shocked (and wildly impressed) that postsecondary institutions, including Harvard, are now emphasizing kindness on applications for admission.[4]

Maybe one of my favorite things about kindness is that it's contagious. See, we're in a constant state of taking cues from those we spend the most time with—our colleagues, our best friends, the other parents on the sports team. It's hard for anyone to be an asshole for long when genuine, kind energy is in the room. And the thing that maybe gets me the most about kindness is that it's memorable.[5] Those "random acts of kindness," even if they aren't acknowledged, are often ingrained very clearly. This whole concept of never underestimating your ability to simply change a life by being kind is honestly a real thing. And although we've probably talked about this enough together, I will reiterate (emphatically for effect this time): You can't tell anyone how to be kind. You just have to show them.

BULLSHIT

"Bullshit," on the other hand, is an interesting word. And because we've learned together that words matter, let's just be clear what we mean by "bullshit." This often-used slang is defined as non-sense, lies, or exaggeration. "Horseshit" apparently is a near synonym, but not quite as strong. "Chicken shit" is more indicative of someone who is not very brave. So, being kind first matters, to get the best out of someone and, ideally, as a segue to ensuring that the prefrontal cortex of another is activated. It doesn't predicate, however, that you're also required to put up with nonsense, particularly if it's untrue or hurtful. So, of all the shits, bullshit is definitely the one we are not interested in tolerating.

Sometimes I worry and have had many long conversations about a misunderstanding in this kindness realm—primarily that kindness means "anything goes." In fact, when trying to work toward a model that is trauma informed and relationship focused in any organization or institution, the idea of leading with kindness can be a paradigm that is, indeed, difficult to sink into. And quite honestly, I'm here for it. I can't tell you the number of debates I've been a part of when I get asked, after a kid has lost their mind, if I'm going to "reward them" with a cookie or by "giving them what they want," including sometimes skipping school altogether so we can get ice cream. The biggest concern, of course, is that we're rewarding the "bad behavior" or that our kindness will be misconstrued as weakness. Further, if we're too kind, others will just walk all over us, and we're left feeling unappreciated or used.

Just to be a hundred million percent clear, sometimes there's no room for kindness first, particularly when violence or safety of another (including yourself) is in play. Then, all bets are off, and demonstrating that safety for them and you is the priority—otherwise nothing good will come. More often than not, however, this truth will remain constant: You can't tell someone how to be kind; you have to lead by example. Kindness is the ultimate lid-flipping-back-oner. Then, and only then, do we start to talk about what needs to happen, how we need to treat each other differently, or what the "consequences" might be.

The one weighing factor that seems to play big into this ability to know when you cross over from Mary Poppins to "don't fucking mess with me" seems to have a lot to do with clarity about what you deserve. There is a clarity that comes with confidence, and I think being clear on who you are and what you "deserve" has so much to do with your ability to be truly vulnerable with your emotions. I know, right? Why does it always come back to that hardest part—trusting each other and ourselves enough to be authentically and vulnerably who we are with other people? Because I'll remind you of that terrible irony that is life. The reason so many of us struggle to be clear on what we deserve and confident enough to go after it or show people who we truly are at our kindest, most vulnerable selves is because someone hasn't been kind to us.

PARADOX

A word on paradox feels right and relevant. Paradox is not an emotion but represents tension between two emotions. The word "paradox" has followed me around lately—and to be honest, I don't really like it. What do you mean that two seemingly contradictory thoughts might be true? And how does this land in this place of trying to understand another person who may be radically different from you? It all, interestingly, comes down to what we can tolerate—our ability to regulate emotion, especially when nothing makes sense. When we struggle with hanging in the midst of paradox, once again we often jump too quickly to "the fix"—to making it all better. I appreciate that pull, that need, that desire. What's interesting to me is that so much of the magic—the learning, growth, insight—happens in the middle of a paradox. Let me explain. As a relationship, however you define it, is coming to an end, it's much easier, often, to become divisive. You are this and I am that. The fact is that is rarely true—or it might all be true but at different times for different people who ascribed different meanings and intentions. The answer lies somewhere in the middle.

Bittersweet might be one of those emotions that represent this paradox idea. You don't have to be one or the other. I have long said that you can have mixed emotions, but one will always have a slight edge—that's typically where we lean when we are in paradox with our emotions. And there are so many experiences that leave us here: our children growing up; the end of a vacation; a divorce; the letting go of friendships that aren't working; or, interestingly, the feeling of nostalgia. So, let's simply say that paradox is hard, good, normal, and so necessary to the most creative and innovative among us. Being kind and not tolerating bullshit seems to be a paradox that is difficult to make sense of sometimes. But when you do that, as often as you're able to and in the order it appears in (kind, first), then the paradox turns into a sequence of events that are in fact not at odds at all.

I think sometimes there's a significant disconnect between being kind (having empathy, even) and the necessity for "take charge" moments. I often see this disconnect in the parenting world. Loving our kids, wanting to avoid their distress, giving everyone a participatory ribbon because we don't want them to have broken hearts is an understandable thing. It's in this thinking that we struggle with boundaries. The necessity to experience full-on heartbreak, loss, and pain for ourselves is hard at best, but to allow others to do that is sometimes unbearable. To not fear it so we can begin to learn where the edges are—of our talent, our authority (or lack thereof), and our safety—is, however, absolutely critical. There's a paradox in this process that I appreciate more and more as the years go by. Turns out, all the same processes apply when we consider adult relationships, too—like when we lead teams or navigate our intimate relationships. I want to dive into this concept of boundaries as we understand just what it means to be both those things—kind and intolerant of bullshit.

BOUNDARIES CAN'T BE BLURRY (AND I HATE THAT)

I've never been a fan of this word "boundaries." I don't even like the sound of the word. It sounds final. And cold. And not very inviting or caring. How can you be a nurturing human who seeks to see the soul of another when you come in with your boundaries all drawn up? In fact, early in my career I was proud of and perhaps even hung my hat on the fact that I had very few boundaries. And by that, I mean you could call me anytime, day or night. I would come back to the hospital to help a nurse put a patient back into bed. I felt compelled to demonstrate to those I served and to my colleagues that I was committed to my work, and for me I thought that meant putting who I served first. I would say even in my friendships I would often forsake what I thought would be good for me just to prove my worth to others.

As I started to develop a platform around connection, boundaries felt like the antithesis to it all. I got the image of somebody standing behind a wall, being very clear that only certain people or ideas are allowed in. That meant you were very good at keeping all the riffraff out. And that didn't make sense to me when I thought about being open and vulnerable, inclusive, and kind. If you wanted to let people see your soul, you had to be kind first and then not tolerate bullshit later. How would boundaries operate to promote that?

It has taken me a long time to believe this statement: Boundaries are a prerequisite for empathy. See, without them, connecting with or serving another quickly morphs into the unclear, messy territory of enmeshment. More specifically, I love boundaries defined as "expectations and needs that help you feel safe and comfortable in your relationships. Expectations in relationships help you stay mentally and emotionally well. Learning when to say no and when to say yes is also an essential part of feeling comfortable when interacting with others."[6]

I also understand how critical boundaries can be in creating and sustaining trust with people. This makes most sense to me when I think about our relationships as parents with our children. In fact, the job for children is often to see how far they can or cannot go with boundaries—that's how they learn where the edges are. If we're unclear about setting boundaries (or unable to hold them) in any roughly predictable fashion, it can be completely debilitating for others to know where they stand. It's most disconcerting, in fact, when those boundaries are unpredictable. In fact, attachment to primary caregivers becomes disorganized or most confusing when those who are to be in charge are unstable or unpredictable (e.g., because of addiction or abuse). The kid doesn't know what to expect or when to expect it, so they tend to live in a constant state of fear, waiting to see if their caregiver is impaired or clear minded.

When I think about the people I've met who have "good boundaries," they often tend to be people I'd consider confident and relatively healthy—meaning they have at least a semi-intact self-esteem and can navigate pushback when someone challenges their boundaries. Further, I guess the relationships where I've been able to establish boundaries most successfully are when I am at my healthiest, most confident. In fact, I now think of boundaries not as walls but as the solid base from which I can jump more confidently into the relationships I foster. This concept is most clear to me when I think about it from the perspective of leading a team.

LEADERSHIP LEGACIES

I struggle the most with boundaries when someone needs my help, particularly when the weight of the world is huge and I feel like I could be doing so much more. I'm not talking about the very clear lines of keeping clients safe; ethically, of course, the clearest lines are always the easiest to follow. It's in the gray areas that so many of us struggle to give our all; it can sometimes feel selfish if we put ourselves first. I became particularly aware of the importance of boundaries when I started to understand how difficult it was for those I was leading to know my expectations if they weren't clear. Even harshly clear. Clear expectations, right out of the gate, is undeniably worth the risk of any hurt feelings. Some of the best employee relationships have worked that way. Will we always have to have conversations when new things arise? Of course. Indeed, clear is kind, and

I've learned the hard way that trying to be kind without clarity can sometimes do far more harm than simply being clear.

In the world of boundaries, one of the greatest teachers is understanding what it feels like when resentment sets in. Resentment is the red flag that a boundary might need to be set (or reset). Let me give you an example. As I started to build my private practice, I often held office hours on weekends and evenings. When I became busier, with three kids at home, I tried to shift to more weekday hours. In fact, I started to resent having to go into the office at 8 PM on a Saturday. I remember, however, that when clients "really needed me," I considered it my ethical responsibility to do whatever I could to accommodate them. To avoid disappointing them or sticking to the narrative in my head that would suggest I needed to be available all the time, I would agree. When 8 PM on Saturday rolled around, however, I could feel the resentment rise. I would show up for the session with no time to spare. I resented the fact that I had agreed to accommodate their schedule (the situation I created). What's interesting is, when I started to be very clear about this idea that there is kindness in clarity, it was so much easier—for me and for them. If I said, "I am so sorry. I wish I could see you on Saturday, but as we discussed, the only times I'm available this week would be Monday at 9 and Wednesday at 4. I hope that you can make either one of those work." Sometimes they'd say, "It will be difficult to make that work, but I will find a way. I'll take Monday at 9." The biggest shift for me: I would show up with my whole heart. And when I noticed that I was better for them because of the boundaries I set, it started to make much more sense. It became the necessary fuel for this understanding: If we're not okay, the people we serve don't stand much of a chance.

BRINGING IT BACK HOME

This little chapter is an important one. Although I believe with my whole heart that kindness is the currency of the next generations, it isn't often understood that the healthiest people among us aren't always "just kind." The healthiest among us understand where the edges are in the relationships that mean the most—and you can't often find these edges until you push up against them. Many of us are on the heels of a generation that suggested we should demand respect before we ever considered the importance of giving fellow humans the benefit of the doubt. Or that respect had to be earned. That behaviorism was predicated on not tolerating bullshit first; then, and only then, could you be kind. Those "best practices," however, were built for a world that no longer exists. We need to build relationships first, in a place where so many relationships don't exist simply because we have so much more space between us. Seeking first to understand before being understood might just be one of the wisest strings of words—first appearing in the Bible according to Luke and later made conventional by educator Stephen Covey.[7] So, keeping in mind this new way of operating in this world, let's consider solidifying a few things before we jump into our final section:

1. Think about the contagious nature of kindness. It can happen in a compliment or a smile. See if you can get it to "catch on."
2. How easy is it for you to be kind these days? Does that change with the seasons or circumstances in your life? And what does it look like when you don't tolerate bullshit (if you have that ability)?

3. What does having "boundaries" mean to you? In which relationships are you better at setting and maintaining these lines?

Part Three

WHEN WE LOSE OUR WAY AGAIN

THREE REVOLUTIONARY RECONNECTION PRACTICES

A reconnection revolution. The word "revolution" may seem a bit aggressive—an oxymoron when written next to the word "relationship" or "reconnection." I do think it's going to take a revolutionary effort to get us back in a state of reconnection to the things that matter most to each of us: our relationships. One more deep breath with me. We've been on quite the journey in these pages. Now what do we do with all the emotion and the hard stuff we've first opened up and then welcomed in and acknowledged? Be damned if I know. Just kidding. I have an idea. When we can maintain connection, especially when things get tough or the challenges come, when we can see people for who they are and have empathy for what they might need—that's when we get the most out of this life. It doesn't mean it's easy—let's just all agree that none of this is fucking easy. But somehow when we have a plan for when it's going to get tough, hope seems a little more like an option.

In fair warning, the "answers" to understanding what it takes to reconnect in a time when it's so much easier not to comes down to some things you might already know. Rarely is ability the biggest concern. Where we get stuck (and stay stuck), however, is accessing those abilities to stay connected to the people and things that matter most to us. The groundwork has been laid. In this final section, we're going to

179

make it sink in a little more deeply and, hopefully, in a memorable way. We'll look at just how much you matter to so many. Which is why, if we don't focus on us first, the rest don't score.

As I sit here with you today, I am the CEO of my own growing company, with 20 employees (almost all of them women). Our primary mission, which not only hangs on the wall but which every single one of these sacred souls embodies, is to reconnect this disconnected world. When I think about (and often marvel at in a state of awe) how—when we first started to really consider our message, this platform, and how I ever had the audacity to think people would want to read what I wrote— it was Marti (who began as a one-day-a-week assistant in my practice and is now our COO) who came up with the word "revolution." And to be honest, we haven't looked back since. Every day that I get to sit with people who are barely hanging on, asking just to be seen, I'm very clear about the necessity of continuing to fight for, speak about, and discuss the importance of a revolution when it comes to relationships. In my privilege, I truly have no concept of what it might be like to be in a revolution. With so many of us battling with few resources left, we will get this wrong, they will get this wrong. Which is why I think a revolutionary effort is what is needed as we step into this final section on reconnection. It won't be an endgame. But knowing we have somewhere to go when it doesn't go just right is all we need.

So many "self-help" books send you off with a list of things that might help to fix the broken relationships around you. But I wanted this one to be different. What I know to be true is that if you're okay, the people you love (and lead, and care for) will have a much better shot at being okay, too. I am reminded of the words of Rumi, the mystic and poet: "Your task is not to seek for love, but merely to seek and find all the barriers within yourself that you have built against it."

The whole reconnection and relationship thing implies that it's all about two people. I think, however, that the answer lies in how we create a world where we reconnect to ourselves first. On purpose and with purpose. The rest, my friends, will follow. We're not good enough, none of us are, to strategically navigate other people to be better and do better. Single-handedly you will not undo systemic oppression or multiple generations of abuse and neglect in the people you love. You (and I) are probably really good, but alone we'll never be powerful enough. The responsibility rests in who we bring to the table. If I'm going to bring my own chair, even on my most exhausted days, I'm going to bring it in and slam that bitch down, saddle up, and strategically sit where others with similar resolve have also claimed their spot.

When you're surrounded by people who have the capacity to acknowledge, you too will continue to rise. It stands to reason, to me anyway, that the best intervention is to create systems that invite these healthy relationships. The only system that we have access to right now, right here in this moment, is you. Staying in the game when doing this hard work of seeing others and not looking away when things get tough isn't necessarily just doing acts of "self-care." I think that's sometimes a cop-out because we can do all the behavioral things and unless our body and our mind are connected, the benefits tend to be superficial. Reconnecting to ourselves has so much more to do with simply feeling all those emotions we've talked about, first, and on purpose. And I'll be completely honest—this is nothing new. We've long known the importance of leaning into the hard stuff. In fact, more than 1,800 years ago, Marcus Aurelius said, "What stands in the way becomes the way." The things we've feared, avoided, tried to go around are often where the answers lie. As we've talked about throughout these pages, the emotions we abhor within ourselves—or others—are often a pretty good indication of where we need to start. Why, if this has always been the answer, is it so hard simply to do it?

"DOING THE WORK"

I've heard reference to "doing the work" so many times, not only as a psychologist but also as a patient. Oftentimes when people struggle, the suggestion so many of us make to the other sounds like "You need to do more work." Or the observation that "he's finally done his work" before he gets into a new relationship indicates he is now ready to be a better, more connected partner. The question for me is really what does "doing the work" mean? How do you know if they've done the work? How do you know if you have done enough work? Or how do you know that somebody else needs to do their work?

This book is, quite frankly, a capturing of me doing my own "work" in real time. It's becoming clear to me that the work happens in the story-telling—in writing the words, for sure, but most importantly in feeling them. In knowing and seeing how emotions take shape in different chapters of your life and that they are not bad—none of them are. Recognizing emotions doesn't happen by coincidence. Holding space for them, inviting them to the table, that is what it means to be doing the work. From a theoretical perspective, I come closest to understanding "doing the work" when I consider the concept of reflective functioning capacity. That concept is defined as the ability to have an awareness of one's own thinking and feelings, while simultaneously being able to have an appreciation for the emotions of others.[1] It involves an increasingly complex awareness that there's more than what's visible on the surface. Most researchers examining someone's reflective functioning capacity have focused on its significance in the context of family systems. As a psychologist, I remember thinking it was easier to work with people who could reflect on their own shit, which meant their defenses were easier to get through. We could do the work of addressing the more vulnerable emotions more quickly. Those were my favorites—the ones who didn't take long to say things like "Okay, I see how I have a role in that"; or "I never thought about it that way. I see how I have contributed to this pattern."

You'll remember, in the early part of this book we talked all about emotional regulation as our foundational ability to stay calm in times of distress. It starts in childhood. The caregiver's capacity to acknowledge and contain emotional experiences demonstrates to the kid how to cope with their own experiences and, in turn, allows them to develop a capacity for concern for others.[2] Absence of emotional containment and the "walking home" part may lead to difficulty integrating emotion and feeling safe to be vulnerable.[3] We do the best we can with what we've got. By relating to other people, we acquire an ability to regulate our own emotions and experiences while staying regulated when faced with the dysregulation of others. As we talked about earlier, the capacity to appreciate our internal state—and that of others—has been found to be essential in developing a concern for others.[4] And emotional understanding and perspective-taking have been found to be precursors of empathic emotions[5] and prosocial behavior.[6] Interestingly, having this capacity aligns quite easily with our ability to do the work or objectively explore our own emotions.

So, what do we do, day to day, that's going to be easy enough to keep us in the game? In this last section, I want to give you a quick game plan—three simple things I lean on every single day. Sometimes I forget just how much I matter to so many. And then, in those quiet moments, I am clear; I don't lose my ability to be the human I want to be, but I often lose access to the best parts of her. It's not so much about fixing the broken parts but knowing how to reconnect to that soul we all came with on this Earth. Those are the skills I think we need to practice on purpose.

Remember back in the beginning of these pages, I talked about how (basically) self-care was bullshit? I may be paraphrasing myself here, but what I mean is that if you don't think you matter in the larger scheme of things, why in the name of all that is holy would you treat the vessel well? So, let's redefine self-care. For me, it means looking inward enough to remember why it's important that you should treat yourself with a little kindness. If there's no reason to, you won't do it well for long. You might be motivated by a wedding-dress fitting, or a challenge on your Apple watch, or the threat of a partner leaving you if you "don't get your shit together and stop drinking." But that won't last if you don't put it into the bigger story you tell yourself.

Sometimes the emotional wave of just feeling it can be more excruciating than any physical pain—which is why so many of us opt out of sinking in, for as long as we can, to the most difficult emotions. There's also something wildly freeing when you just surrender to feelings, knowing those feelings can't kill you and that, indeed, feeling them is the way home. Sometimes, so many times, that's all you need. Somewhere, someone, something to just hold it all for a while. And when you put the load down, if only for a few moments, you pick it up again differently. It might be all the same stuff, but what you do with it matters. Little shifts in the load, particularly if you can share it with someone, somehow makes it more manageable. That's where we start to make sense of it— when we start to make meaning out of the mess. It's not the experiences that happen to us, it's what we do with them that matters.

Now—let's be clear—this is not your "fault" when you hit a chapter or a whole life where you don't appear to be "handling it well." Too often, I think, we get into this space where we believe someone is clearly not strong enough if they can't get to the vulnerable parts of their soul. And to be honest, there is a component of choice and willingness. But for some of us, there are seasons or even lifetimes where it is harder. Trauma, marginalization, the amount of shit you have on your plate at any given time will make it more difficult to just "put down" for a while. So, as always, there is grace in that process, too. The goal here, dear ones, is to understand that the lessons then become teachers instead of burdens. The experiences don't change, but how you hold them does. And you start to live again, even if it's just a little.

One more solidifying fact indicating that this whole "doing life" thing is, indeed, really fucking hard is that you never arrive. There is, I've discovered, no magical place where even the best of them who appear to have it all together ever stay for long. It's a constant journey of reconnection that is the whole reason we are here. For me, although there could be multiple chapters on the intricacies of reconnection, it really is simple. So I'm going to do my best to make it that way here. This last section of these sacred pages is all about how, in just three never-ending practices of reconnecting, we can become the beacons, the game-changers, the healthiest of all in this charge to reconnect a disconnected world. You are the most important part.

As Rumi explains, "The cure for pain is in the pain." I really don't love that. At all. But it's true. Involved in all this process, as you can well understand, are repeated connections, disruptions, and reconnections that allow us to firmly develop our skills of not only regulating our own emotion but then, importantly, being able to reflect on those of others and on how we contribute to that dynamic. The word "reconnection" becomes synonymous with that process, and it has become the mantra of the work so many of us, when we are at our best, are doing well. So, how do we get this world to work together toward reconnection? I think it might just be time for a revolutionary effort that starts right here, with you and me.

I don't think the answer lies in how we learn the "strategies" to be better, and do better, for others. The answer lies, I think, in a simple roadmap that reconnects us to, and grounds us within, ourselves when emotions start to push us around. Then, and only then, will we have access to our best abilities to give away our most authentic self and be the spark that offers the light in the darkest corners. If we skip to fixing, helping, or caring for others, we will lose our way. That is where resentment and divisiveness live and where we so often find ourselves, and each other, these days. So, you and I, we are the answer. I am so hopeful that we have all we need to change the world in our lifetimes. In fact, I think if we only knew just how powerful we are, we'd step in with our whole hearts just a little more often. We are the priority and where "the work" must always start.

We have three stops in this final section. First, reconnecting to your people, and we will define "your people" clearly. Second, reconnecting to your breath by dropping those shoulders. And finally, stepping back from time to time to take in the bigger picture. These three happen, for me, often in the order we're going to talk about them, although any one of them is as powerful as the other two. These, as you'll notice, are not about how you connect to others. You are, in fact, very good at that part. I promise. If and when we look after you first, when your heart is full, your confidence is high, your competence is feeling strong—then you are at your best and you are more open to this connection thing. You are your best self, parent, partner, employee, leader when we look after you first. The richest parts of our lives live in the spaces where we are whole enough to see the best in others and to allow ourselves to be seen. So let's end this book with the practices that make you (and me) our first priority.

CHAPTER TEN

Practice 1—Your People

SIT WITH THE WINNERS . . . THE CONVERSATION IS DIFFERENT

The people you surround yourself with, if you invest in them well, will become the village that walks with you through the successes, carries you through the shadows, and takes you to task when you need a wake-up call. It never ceases to amaze me that the ones who are most able to look and see seem to be the ones who have created the most solid safety nets around them. Now, this notion of keeping your people close isn't a new one. It's a universal truth that we are wired for connection and that we were never meant to do this alone. It seems like the biggest challenge is remembering to do just that—to invest the time to not only look but to see the ones who matter the most to us. Although we can appreciate that this investment in the people closest to us makes the most sense, it also seems, sometimes, like the most difficult thing to do. There's a reason why, right out of the gate, we will revisit the importance of reconnecting to your people. And although it's interesting that we need this reminder, the hardest thing you and I have on our plates this moment is looking into the eyes of the people who matter the most to us. So, let's start there— with the most powerful tool that we often mess up the most.

YOUR PERSON(S)

"Your people," the ones who truly know you—not with a title or by your accomplishments, but by your heart and your story—are the ones whose opinions should hold the most weight. There are others of course we will talk about, but let's start there, at the core. I will tell you about my *Grey's Anatomy* obsession phase. I basically became an MD during these years of commitment to the first 12 seasons—and I can tell you, in Season 8, Episode 24, when Meredith says to Cristina, "You are my person. You will always be my person," I remember thinking just how lucky they were to have each other. I've had a few "my persons" throughout my days. Those are the most sacred ones. And we need to know who they are.

By virtue of the fact that you're going to *reconnect* to them, it tells us you've had a relationship with this person or these people before. It's precisely why the connection to new people is often the easiest part. As we talked about earlier, it's why affairs are easy, it's why you know second dates come much more emotionally charged than the 154th date after 14 years together and three kids on the ground. It's about the ones who truly know your soul that dictates your health, your worth, or your ability to be great in this world. It's knowing that you have a place to land when things go sideways that keeps us the healthiest. So it would stand to reason that our energy should be directed there, as often as we're able. There likely aren't very many who can, or should, hold that title.

With all that in mind, if you're trying to decide who would fit the highest honor of meeting the criteria of being your person, here are a few things I consider when making my list. First, if a bra or makeup is required, they're likely not your people. If you have said anytime in the last few months "Oh, they didn't invite me" (to golf, or to the game, or to some other event and it bothered you because you were deliberately left out, with no explanation), those, my friends, are also not your people. Instead, think about the people who come to mind the easiest when you consider who you would trust to sit on your kitchen floor with a pile of laundry, snot everywhere, crying your eyes out. Who could hold that? In fact, who has held that degree of emotional dysregulation before and most notably didn't flinch? Belly laughter is also another defining criterion in the making of my list. Honesty is encouraged, and vulnerability isn't scary. Sometimes our own untold or unacknowledged trauma histories don't allow us to feel safe enough to allow others in. But if you have been, and are able, to let in any human close to you, notice the ones who leave you feeling stronger shortly after a departure. Conversely, if you're not a crier or much of a talker, consider the list of people who you would be completely comfortable with if you just showed up at their house, grabbed a beer, and sat on a lawn chair, with nobody saying anything for as long as three hours.

Now, unless you're a phenomenal connector, the list of people who would meet those criteria typically isn't massive. I want you to really think about who knows you. Who has, if even briefly, seen behind all those walls and defenses we set up to try to make sure that people think we're doing okay or we're fine? Has anyone ever given pause after they've asked the question, "But really, how are you?" Oftentimes, with these select few, there is a genuineness that you can feel from the parking lot. Not an "I want to gather information to see if you're more fucked up than me" kind of a comparative feeling, but "I want you to be okay because I deeply care for you" genuine kind of feeling. For me, this list of people has shifted over time. Although there are a solid three who haven't wavered since I started being clear on who made the cut, I also think sometimes the more we're hurt, and we don't address those hurts, it becomes difficult to do the work with the ones who know us the deepest.

DEATH ENDS A LIFE, NOT A RELATIONSHIP

As you are considering who's on the list for you, I want to tell you it has occurred to me recently that sometimes your person can remain one of your persons even if they're no longer on this planet. One of my favorite quotes is by sportswriter and author Mitch Albom, who in his heartwarming true story *Tuesdays with Morrie*,[1] says this: "Death ends a life, not a relationship." Is it possible, I started to really wonder, even if someone was your person and they die, could they still be your person? I know they can, because I have one.

Let me tell you about my Rhea. We were first neighbors in college residence and then roommates our second year. Rhea knew the stories of the darkest chapters of my life, including when my parents finally divorced during that second year of college. Rhea told me years later that she remembered the phone calls home, the confusion, the tears, the conversations, the worries for my mom. I remember very little about that year, mostly because I didn't want to. And because she was able to hold so much of it for me, she was the one—the only one—who could fill in the gaps when I wasn't able to. She could make me laugh like no other. And the jokes that meant something only to us—the Ukrainian cooking afternoons when we wore babushkas, the Kenny and Dolly Christmas album, and many a road trip with stories that will stay on the road. I gave the toast to the bride at her wedding; we rocked each other's babies to sleep; she sat in many of the first audiences I had when I started to speak about the things you're reading here. And I gave the eulogy at her funeral. Rhea lost her battle to cancer in 2019, leaving behind two babies and a beautiful husband. And what the fuck was I supposed to do without one of my persons?

As I sit here on this snowy day, I realize that I spoke so much about Rhea when I knew it was likely we were going to lose her. She was still here, physically, when I wrote my first book. She had just died when I wrote the second. And now it's been three years. And maybe this is something we can't really know until the people we love die. And I have to tell you, it wasn't until after she'd been gone for a few months that I realized I check in with her more now than time would allow when she was here.

I'll tell you one quick story. Just recently, one of the biggest moments of my career happened. I have a list of five people who I'd love to meet before I die, and she knew it. And I didn't just want to meet these five—I want to collaborate with, dream with, know them. So, here's my list. The first is Ron MacLean (Canadian hockey god). I think he's so smart, and we could talk hockey for days. The second is Dr. Brené Brown, researcher and social worker goddess (who I've referenced the heck out of in this book, you might have noticed). The third would be Shonda Rhimes—brilliant writer (of *Grey's Anatomy* and so much more). Fourth is the impeccable Oprah Winfrey, because, well, she's the queen. And last (but the list is in no particular order) is writer and all-around sacred badass Elizabeth Gilbert. Now just last month, I gave an opening talk—and guess who I opened for? Number five—Liz Gilbert—and she Blew. Me. Away. At first, I fumble-fucked my way through a gushing introduction, tried to ask her about her recent talk that I thought was in Denver (turns out it was in Portland), and did a lot of nodding because it felt safer than to open my mouth. Then, in the quiet green room, I sat with her, had dinner, and truly understood what it means to sit with the winners. The conversation was different. And the entire time I was losing my mind (on the inside).

I tried to breathe through her references to learnings from Brené, and Martha Beck, and Rob Bell (all people who have instrumentally shaped my career). I told her about this book. When it was time for me to go on stage she said, "Go kill it, Jody. I'll be watching." *What?* I said, "Elizabeth Gilbert, that might be the most frightening fucking sentence I have ever heard in my career." She laughed and said, "Just go tell your story, dear one. It's all any of us have."

At the end of my talk (I did kill it) and hers, I couldn't wait to just soak it all in and make sense of everything. And you know who I desperately wanted to tell? My Rhea. So, I snuck up to the hotel room and went out on the balcony. I opened my arms to the sky and said, "Did you see that?" And she answered in my soul, as she always does, "Hell, yeah, I did! You fucked it up there in the beginning, but you pulled it together perfectly, JC." Ahh, friends. She was right. And I am reminded always, and in all ways, that we are never alone.

See, in the moments when we need to reconnect the most, it's often the people who have meant the most to us, even if we didn't allow ourselves to fully know it when they were here, who seem to guide us when they're gone. Sometimes I feel it more strongly than other times. But I do think that there is a picture way bigger than us and, when I believe that to be true, it takes the pressure off. And it feels powerful to believe that we are guided, if we allow it, by our ancestors and the other people who came before us.

I am reminded of Maya Angelou's words when she read her poem "On the Pulse of Morning" at President Bill Clinton's first inauguration. She went back to the very beginning of the First Peoples who inhabited what is now called America, incanting the names of the Apache, the Seneca, the Cherokee, and the Sioux, gathering as well the names of other "passed on traveller[s],"the Ashanti, the Yoruba, and the Kru, as well as the Turk, the Swede, the German, and the Scot. Later, in an interview about that day, she said she could feel the ancestors there with her on stage. She surmised that she never felt alone when she was on stage because she had her ancestors walking with her. And ever since, Rhea and all those who have come before me are the ones who are with me whenever I get to deliver words I hope will heal.

This whole "it takes a village" thing is real. And although being very clear who your persons are is the biggest message here, I also want to draw your attention to the company you keep on a broader scale. Although it seems wiser and wiser to pay attention to the ones whose opinions matter the most, we are inevitably making choices every day about who to sit with, what information to consume, who to read, and who to follow—choices that significantly dictate how we show up. Find the others who share your resolve. And know what your people in any specific group will tolerate—and, most importantly, promote. If treating people unkindly is "okay" behind closed doors, or around the fire pit when "no one is listening," you can never be too confident where those boundaries will bend. And what I've considered most recently is that who I choose to surround myself with sends a clear message to others, including my children, of what I deem acceptable. What you permit, you promote. And here's the cool part: You can re-evaluate these choices with each new learning and each new season of your life.

IT'S REAL TO FEEL

I want to make one thing so clear: It's not about becoming numb to the feedback of others to protect your heart. Feedback is critical if we ever hope to grow, particularly feedback from those who are not like you. And be clear on whose opinion about the most important parts of your character really matters. In *Rising Strong*,

Brené Brown writes: "When we stop caring what people think, we lose our capacity for connection. But when we are defined by what people think, we lose the courage to be vulnerable."² Take feedback gratefully and always have someone to check it with. Pay close attention to the stuff that feeds your soul, inspires you to think differently, and, even if it hurts, leaves you wanting to be better.

Physicist Richard P. Feynman is known for saying that if you are the smartest person in the room, then you're in the wrong room. Some of my most inspiring moments are when I can look around a table and know that I have so much to learn from so many. I feel that when I sit with elders or other people who are willing to share their knowledge of the things I know nothing about. It doesn't mean they must be more educated than you; in fact, I've learned the most from people who have no letters behind their names. Kids in particular, my kids, and the ones I've sat with in therapy offices, tend to be the greatest teachers.

RELATIONSHIP KNOWS NO HIERARCHY

I started saying these words—relationship knows no hierarchy—after spending a lot of time with teachers in K–12 education. In many of our organizations there is a clear delineation between who's at the top and who's at the bottom of the workplace hierarchy. And when we started talking about what kids need, particularly the ones who struggle in our schools these days, it was clear to me that the ones who need to feel seen the most are the hardest to give it to. And when someone needs to be acknowledged, no one, including kids, cares about credentials. They just want to know, genuinely, that they matter. In fact, some of the most connected relationships know no race, religion, socioeconomic status, age, ability, or gender identity. We tend to spend most of our time with people who look like us, sound like us, even smell like us. But some of the richest relationships are found in the ones where we learn about how much we are alike, especially when we are so different. Let me tell you a story about Old Bill and a boy named Asher.

Picture Asher as a slightly awkward, bright, anxious fifth grader. He's in a new school and there was a desperation, for all involved, for this kid to make some friends. On a Wednesday afternoon, a few weeks into the school year, Asher burst through the door at the end of the day, announcing to anyone who'd listen that he "made a new friend." The question was asked about this new friend's name. "Old Bill," Asher announced proudly. Clarification was provided, and it turns out that Old Bill was 92. Asher had met him on his walk home from school, when Old Bill commented on the boy's vocal skills as he sang to himself going past Bill's house. Having been paid a compliment, Asher stopped and struck up a conversation. In fact, he later explained that he sat up on Old Bill's deck for a bit, learning his age and that he was a teacher in a "former life" and had five children. Asher explained that he'd been stopping by to have a chat with Old Bill, who waited for him most days after school, for the past week.

Asher is my son and, at the first light of this story, there were concerns about Old Bill. "Did you go into his house? What did he say to you?" It makes me sad that my first response wasn't pride, but fear. I shared my concerns with Asher, and he said, "I thought you might feel that way, Mom. Let's go meet him together tomorrow." The next day, any concerns were quickly swept away when, after school, Asher led me to Old Bill's house to meet him. Bill told me that he was honored to meet me and that he was so impressed with our young man. He wanted Aaron and me to be sure that he was "safe" and was very proud to have a friend like Asher. He had taught Asher's grandmother in school and then, I have to tell you, I was so grateful to be living in a small town where everyone seems to know a lot about each other. I was reminded just how much it takes a village—and trusting in it can be tricky, even dangerous at times. But at that moment, I felt nothing but blessed. It also made me starkly aware that this is all I ever hoped for my kids—that they would do their very best to connect, genuinely, to people.

That day, Old Bill invited us in for ice cream. As the three of us enjoyed black cherry ice cream (Bill's favorite, Asher told me) on a sunny September day, I watched my son and this 92-year-old great-grandfather have a conversation about humanity that took my breath away. And months later, when Bill's health began to fail, we all held our breath. The visits continued and we designated Mondays and Wednesdays as the stop-by-after-school days, as long as Bill was up for it. And then one day just before Christmas, Asher came home with a big wooden box. He said, "Old Bill gave this to me today." He opened it up and he showed me a microscope that had been Bill's when he taught biology for 40 years at the high school. He told Asher, "I want you to have this. It's very special to me. And so are you." Our son's best friend was 92.

This world lost Old Bill peacefully two weeks later. His daughter was kind enough to let us know, as his children and grandchildren knew of Bill's friendship with Asher. Telling our son that Old Bill died was one of the hardest moments in our parenting careers. Aaron took the lead but couldn't choke out the words through his own tears, so the three of us just hugged and cried. Most nights, I still hear Asher say good night to Bill in his prayers. Old Bill taught this mama and our boy that, indeed, relationship knows no hierarchy.

LETTING THEM KNOW

The people we love the most are suspicious when we're kind. I think it's the ultimate evidence of disconnect. In fact, let's run a little experiment right here. I've done this many times when I've spoken with live audiences. Pause wherever you are, reading these words, and take out your phone (if you have one). Next, choose one of your persons. If I can be so bold, I would recommend you choose someone you are intimately involved with. Preferably somebody you're married to, particularly if your relationship is in a tricky stage. Ooh—and if you've procreated with somebody and are no longer married, you could even pick them—it's a risky choice but often it will pay off. If you have no one in your life who fits into that partner category at this moment, choose someone who you know needs to reconnect with you today. How will you know they need that? Just sit quietly for a moment and notice who floats into your head.

Now, on your phone (or on a note if that's easier), pull up that person you were thinking about and text these words: "I don't know if I tell you this enough, but you matter to me." And hit Send. If you didn't follow the directions and just kept reading, stop and do it now. I mean it, dammit.

I can predict that a few things are going to happen—there are some very common responses in the moments following this directive. A significant number of you will likely get a phone call immediately from the texted party, asking, "Are you okay?" And some of my other favorite immediate text responses include things like: "Was this meant for me?" "Are you sure you texted the right person?" And "LOL" always gets me. Even though I've sent a few of these to my husband over the years, Aaron has often texted this back to me: "What did you buy?"

Further, please don't panic if your loved one doesn't respond immediately—they're probably in shock. Just kidding. Not really kidding. But seriously, if there is no response, they may truly be unable to get to their phones. Sometimes we don't trust this kind of message, so it's not safe to respond immediately (or ever). This is actually a perfect time for that wall to go up because we're vulnerable when we say the things we sometimes feel and don't get the response we expect. That experience of rejection often results in a withdrawal. When we experience a physical blow, like a literal gut punch, we don't say, "Come at me again!" It's a primitive reaction, and it makes sense. However, if you can wait, the payoff is usually a vulnerable moment.

And if the person you texted asks if someone told you to send them this message, I want you to lie. I don't want you to say, "Oh, don't worry about it, I was just reading an amazing book by Jody Carrington who gave me the direction to send this to you." Don't you dare say that. You lie! And you say, "No [insert term of endearment], I was just thinking about you today." Deal?

What I want you to notice more than anything is what that response is like. So many of you will get back "You too, honey"; or "Thanks for that. You matter to me, too." For others, if you can withstand the first shock or surprise or "do you really mean it?" kind of question, what you will see is they're just making sure it's safe. That it was meant for them. And when they get confirmation that the intention of the message was indeed genuine, you will likely receive it in return—or at the very least, there will be a softening. And therein lies the importance of the reconnection to your people.

Now I will say that, once again, women tend to be better at this reconnection thing than men. For example, I've heard many times in my office a female-identifying partner say, "I'm always the one who has to initiate these things." Or, "Why do I always have to apologize first?" And we start to assume that our partner doesn't want to or doesn't feel that way, or a myriad of other explanations about why we always must be "the one." First, I would say there's often a selection bias that happens in our memories which contributes to believing we're always the one who does the work. But I'll tell you it's not that men (or those who identify as having a masculine energy) don't have feelings. But as we talked about in the earlier chapters, one of the superpowers of those with some emotional language is being better at sorting out the suspicious defenses. That's what's often required in the reconnection piece—being able to bravely, vulnerably, reach out to the people you love the most and make it safe to let the walls down and be seen, even if just for a bit, every now and then.

BOTTOM HANDS ONLY—
THE REST DON'T SCORE

Here's the other really cool thing about your persons. You're rarely too something for them. You're rarely too loud or too quiet or too over the top or too big or too small. I think so many of us spend a lot of our life trying to be something for somebody else. And although I struggle with this some days because critical feedback matters, I spend a lot of my time trying to figure out whose feedback is critical.

In *Kids These Days*[3] I introduced this concept of the bottom hands. It comes from a theory that John Bowlby[4] proposed about attachment, noting that primary caregivers play two roles in regulating emotion in their children: They act as both a secure base and a safe haven. The secure base represents the need in relationships to have someone to lean on who makes it safe enough to step out into the world and take risks. When we doubt ourselves, these are the times we need someone to cheer us on (or kick us in the proverbial ass) and say, "I've got you. Keep going." It's where we begin to learn from experience that we can do hard things. Equally important in a relationship is needing a safe place to land when, not if, life gets hard. Bowlby called those experiences our "safe havens."

Since Bowlby's original theory, many researchers and clinicians, including Glen Cooper and colleagues of the Circle of Security model,[5] depicted this need for a secure base and a safe haven in a diagram that looked like hands on the circle. Imagine cupping your hands, joined at your wrists to make a circle. They explained that, ideally, the role of a primary caregiver is to act as "hands on the circle" for kids. In the most secure relationships, big people act as the cheerleader when their kids need to take risks, pushing them out to the top of the circle and being the safe place to land when life gets hard. And we travel around and around that circle frequently. That top hand serves as the place to gently support kids or the other people you love as they need the confidence to go into the world. Having someone in your corner who says things like "you've got this" or "I believe in you" is so critical when you don't believe in yourself or don't have the experience or the script to confirm that, indeed, you can "do it." No doubt when you're out on that circle doing great things in this world, your heart is going to get bruised, making mistakes is a given, and you're going to feel all the things like shame, regret, remorse, fear, and disappointment. Cooper and colleagues suggest that we will need someone with a "bottom hand" to catch us when we fall—someone to organize our feelings and calm us down. Once again, the deal is not to avoid these heavy feelings. But the healthiest among us will have somewhere to land when, not if, the safe haven is needed.

I really love this concept of hands on the circle when we consider who our people are. In particular, the concept of bottom hands became a condensed version of considering who really matters to me and something I've talked about to many audiences. When you're thinking about your persons, I want you to consider who your bottom hands are. Like when your heart is particularly broken, and you go through the list of people you could call and know instantly that one feels just right. Sometimes the ones you choose in a crisis surprise you. Sometimes you just know to be true that they're the ones who will get you. They may not even have the right words to bring you home, but they feel like home.

I told the story of one such "bottom hand" in *Kids These Days*—a woman I met early in my speaking career. Let me set the stage again here, because she remains someone who I think about often when the critics come calling.

I was asked to speak at a conference in a large city. This was an exciting opportunity, on a big stage. As I navigated my way into this new world of speaking, figuring out how to deliver my message authentically, there was a lot (and I mean a lot) of conversation about how much I swear. I heard often that my message was important, but "we would rather that you deliver it in a way that is easier to hear." Or, "Jody, is it possible that you don't swear?" I've always said the same thing: "Of course I can 'not swear.' I have that ability. I'm a bright and articulate woman." I've also struggled with remaining authentic. Now I was standing at this conference wondering how you navigate this quest for authenticity while being in a place where you sincerely don't want to offend people. How do you avoid putting yourself into the boxes of other people's expectations simply to appease them? And, for the record, I feel that women have done that for multiple generations.

On the day of the big keynote, I was standing, sipping my coffee, when the organizer of the event came over to me 10 minutes before I was to take the stage. He said, nervously, as he tugged at his suit jacket, "The committee has just talked one more time and they're really concerned that you will be swearing today." And a few things simultaneously went through my head. First of all, I thought we had an understanding about who you were hiring and how I deliver my message. We also had the conversation that I would be respectful in this regard and explain how I show up in the world. And why are you giving me this warning minutes before I go on? Not the best time for feedback, dude! And maybe, most importantly, the doubt flooded in, and I started to wonder if the way I showed up in the world was just too much.

As I was considering the costs of stepping out the door, this most beautiful soul came over to me. She said, "Dr. Carrington, can I talk to you real quick?" And I thought, "Oh, God, here we go." We chatted briefly about why she was at this conference for educators when she explained she was not a teacher. But her husband was. I asked her where he taught now, and she told me it was "a long story." When I said, "Tell me more," my heart broke as she explained that her husband had been killed in a car accident two years earlier, along with their 10-month-old daughter. She and her two sons had been in the vehicle and had survived. Every single day, she explained, she was struggling to live well for them and to serve her husband's and her daughter's legacy. She told me she had heard me speak a few months back and was reminded that she was wired to do hard things. She told me her favorite parts were that I was "real" and, most importantly (at least how I remember it), that I swore—because she finally listened. Those were the words that grabbed her. She told me that since that day, she was able to look at the hardest time in her life and still be able to smile sometimes. She said to me, "Keep doing what you're doing. It's changing people. And promise me you'll never dull your light." And that was the moment a bottom hand was born. She didn't know it that day, but because of her I got up on that stage and poured my heart out— with all the things that I thought could save the babes who every single person in that audience influenced every day. With swear words laced throughout for inflection when I felt, authentically, the message required it. And you know what? I got my first standing ovation.

I wanted her to know just how much her husband's and her daughter's legacies were alive in the words she was brave enough to share with me. Since that day, we have spent time together on a few occasions. She was at the launch of *Kids These Days*, and I love watching this mama raise her two incredible boys. She since has explained to me more details of the day her sweet husband Colin and their daughter Madeline died. This story continues to fuel my passion for authenticity, particularly when I need it the most. To be honest, I swear less these days because I've considered my pushback might be because when people tell me I can't do something, I want to do it even more. Regardless, I'm clear that even if you do all the things, you won't be just right for everybody. That's the hard part, see, because so many of us just want people to like us. As you navigate the next few days and weeks (maybe even years), I want you to know, when you consider who your bottom hands might be, your job is to play to the ones who believe in you, the ones who will catch you when you fall. This little rule hasn't failed me yet: Bottom hands only. The rest don't score.

SPEND IT WISELY

One last thing I'll say about reconnecting with your people is this: So many of us who serve other humans in our communities—whether as first responders, parents, community service providers, teachers, clerks, cashiers, or even therapists—we are all just here walking each other home. As you might recall, when you think about reconnecting not just to your persons but to all those in your circle, I want you to consider a rank order for where you put your very sacred and often limited energy. You matter the most and, from there, consider it a three-step process. First, spend the most amount of reconnection energy on the people who are in the house where you wake up every morning. The people closest to you deserve the best from you. The ones you consider your persons fit in here, too. Second, if you're employed outside the home (even if you work from home), pour whatever resources you have leftover into your team, your colleagues, your coworkers—the people you work beside. It's so much easier to commit to a profession when you feel like you're part of a team. And finally, last but not least, the people you serve: your clients, students, customers, patients. We're often most worried about the people we serve, but if those closest to us aren't okay, the people we serve don't stand a chance.

BRINGING IT BACK HOME

Your people. They all dance in and out of different circles that surround you as you walk through this life. Those closest to you, your sacred few, your persons, are often the ones you forget to give your best to—because they mean so much that it makes it difficult to do; or you're concerned they won't reciprocate it; or you simply take them for granted; or a combination of all these. And because we're social creatures, the healthiest among us are the most socially integrated in our communities. Pay close attention to who you're sitting with and never, ever forget your power, regardless of where you "fall" in any given hierarchy (self-ascribed or by the title you hold). I hope you do indeed have a lot of friends but, it turns out, a select few get us through this life. Get the ones in your head who truly know your story. Those who have had the most access to your soul, underneath any hurt and trauma and pain that we all have gathered at some points in our story. Those are your people. Connect to one of them daily, if you're able to. A text, a note, a prayer is simply all you need. The truth is, the people we love the most are often suspicious when we're kind. For this reason, we need to reconnect with our people as often as we're able to. It will take a conscious effort in this season of heaviness. And it is a powerful antidote to it all.

1. Make a list, on paper or in your head, of the specific few in your life who you would identify as your persons. Remember, this list can change over the years. But who makes you belly laugh, knows your middle name, and would take a call in the middle of the night? They're rare and they're sacred.

2. Who are you surrounding yourself with the most these days? If you want clues, look at who you follow most often on social media, or who you spend time coordinating schedules to see. Just notice how it makes you feel after you spend time with them or in the spaces they create. Decide today who might have to go.

3. Relationship knows no hierarchy. This is your gentle reminder to reach beyond relationships with people who are most like you. See what you can learn about someone who doesn't fit with your expectations of who people should be.

CHAPTER ELEVEN

Practice 2—Drop Those Shoulders
That Mind-Body Reconnection

I originally used the words "reconnecting to your breath" as the title of this chapter so it would be easy to remember. But I realized that often before I'm ready to take a deep breath, it helps if I first simply notice where my shoulders are (often, or at least every time I've ever checked, they are firmly secured to my earlobes). The cue for this practice is simply to drop them. Getting back to a place of connection between your body and your mind seems easiest for me when I just drop my shoulders. Then, if you're able, proceed with that slow, easy, deep breath. This seemingly woo-woo top-three practice is the one that's taken me the longest to get comfortable with. I'm not good just "sitting" with my breath (or relaxing my body, turns out) for long. I've got shit to do! And if I'm being truly honest, if I sit still long enough, I'm afraid of what I might feel.

Here's the thing, the data around this mind-body connection thing is far from woo-woo. In fact, some of the strongest scientific support for mental health lives in the critical connection between your head and your heart[1] and the need to consciously step out of the spin. Most of us are familiar with the spin—the chaos that feels more like home than the calm. And if not the spin, the necessity to be doing something, anything other than resting, meant that you were doing "work." I grew up with the message that if you're not constantly busy, you're lazy—and it's a hard message to shake. I often wonder about where this came from, this chronic need to perform and accomplish. One of the most common responses I give and often hear to the question of "how are you?" is "so busy." In fact, my long-time favorite combination of words, just to make it clear that I've a lot on the go, is, "I'm crazy-busy." It almost feels like a competition sometimes; we justify our worth by the number of things we accomplish on the list every day. Paying close attention to how we describe our day matters. Gandhi said, "Your words become your actions, your actions become your habits." These days, I'm trying these words on for size a little more often: "clear," "fulfilled," "hopeful," or "overwhelmed" instead of "just busy." Whatever fits for you can significantly shift how you show up in the world and be fodder for meaningful conversations. In fact, the antithesis, deeply rooted in spiritual practices, tends to be the opposite of the spin. In prayer, reflection, meditation, mindfulness, there is a necessity for slowing down and being still.[2] And sometimes, when things get really difficult, being spiritually connected is the only thing we have left.

IT'S SPIRITUAL

When plagues or famines, death or war, hit, people turn to the spiritual practices or lean heavily into their religion to cope. When uncertainty is upon us, people pray for and depend on one another. When terror tries to steal life from us, if we are at all able, we stand in solidarity and hope for the goodness of humanity. There is divisiveness between whatever or whoever has caused the pain and those on the receiving end. The (necessary) result is often a banding together in something bigger to get through it. The National Alliance on Mental Illness states that "spirituality also incorporates healthy practices for the mind and body, which positively influences mental health and emotional well-being." As we discussed earlier, the mental health of many has sunk to the lowest measurable point in history. The only group to see (albeit slight) improvements in mental health during the first year of the pandemic was those who attended religious services at least weekly (virtually or in person).[3] Science is a very valuable part of humanity; however, it hasn't yet explained it all. And when things are uncertain, we're scared. And when there's no end in sight, we need somewhere to put it.

Important to note, I think, is that although these terms are sometimes used interchangeably, religion and spirituality are two very different things. And the gap between the two may be more profound today than ever. Religion and spirituality are both rooted in attempts at comprehending the meaning of life and, in some cases, how a relationship with a higher power or a more profound plan may influence that meaning. Religion is an organized, community-based system of beliefs, while spirituality resides within the individual.[4] Religion rarely exists without spirituality; however, spirituality doesn't necessarily involve religion. Further, religion as a construct has long been plagued with misogyny, patriarchy, and widespread abuse by religious authorities who have significantly damaged the major premise of purity and love.[5] I think what is critically vital in this practice of dropping your shoulders is that it tends to trigger on a deeper, even neurophysiological, level the necessity to call in the calm. See, it's impossible to take a deep breath and have a flipped lid simultaneously. It's so often why we tell distressed people to "take a deep breath." Although that direction is sometimes followed, it's often most effective when someone else demonstrates the calm—showing how to get there and not just telling. The truth is that anxiety can't live in a calm body.

If you're not prepared for a deep dive into spirituality and all the conquests that surround it, I offer you this. I heard Oprah say that she didn't even like the word "meditation," so she just went with the word "stillness" instead. Remember it's a practice. In many moments while writing these words for you, I went still, hoping to be clear on what words might need to land on these pages. I can tell you, it's there for the taking whenever we slow down long enough to invite it in.

LET'S DO IT TOGETHER

Now, if you're so inclined, put a little sticky note on this page, because my guess is you might need this section a lot over the days ahead as we navigate all the emotion there is in the world. I want you to start by simply dropping your shoulders. If you can, envision the tension melting away. Follow that with a deep breath; slow, easy, relaxed—but as deep as you can. Sometimes at the exhale of that deep breath your shoulders might drop just a little more. And that's just what we want. Next, relax your jaw. Drop your tongue from the roof of your mouth. It's interesting, but it's a very primitive response to slam your tongue to the roof of your mouth when in a state of heightened arousal. So, relax your jaw and drop that tongue. Next, if you're able, wiggle your toes. This simply brings into awareness your entire body. And finally, let your gut out. Don't laugh, just do it! Particularly for women, we spend a lot of time convincing ourselves that we're relaxed while we're simultaneously sucking in. For the record, you cannot be relaxed and sucking in at the same time. Also for the record, you're beautiful and perfect, especially when you give yourself permission to relax. This sequence of getting back into your body is a shortcut I use quite often to get grounded. And I will tell you, I don't come by it naturally. In fact, on the toughest days, I put an alarm on my phone to go off a few times; just a simple reminder to drop my shoulders. And every time I get that reminder, you can guess where my shoulders are. Every time.

So, just for fun, do that little sequence again. Shoulders, breath, jaw, tongue, toes, gut. For even more effect, smile. There you go. Now do you feel that, my friend? That, right there, is a relaxed body. And we don't spend a lot of time there. Lately, we've been in a heightened state of arousal more often. And furthermore, many of us have come from multiple generations where it was safer to expect the worst and were taught to have a plan for any impending disaster so you'll be ready for anything. We've had many messages, either overt or subtle, that would suggest you should never get too cocky. The thought was that if you weren't prepared for the fall from joyous reveling and unprepared frolicking, it would be high and harsh. Many of us, inherently, feel much safer in a place of complaining than in a place of truly sinking into gratitude. Some call this foreboding "joy."[6]

GET ON THE GRATITUDE TRAIN

So, let's talk about this concept of gratitude, since you brought it up. It's a commonly prescribed exercise in my business. "Practice some gratitude" and you will be a much happier person, dammit. The truth is that people who have the capacity to lean fully into joy have one variable in common: They practice gratitude.[7] Turns out, however, it's a bit harder to do than you may think. See, gratitude practice is just that—it's a practice. It works better if you do it. And it works better if you do it more often. By definition (the one I like the best, anyway), gratitude is "an emotion that reflects our deep appreciation for what we value, what brings meaning to our lives, and what makes us feel connected to ourselves and others."[8]

More grateful people are happier, more satisfied with their lives, less materialistic, and less likely to suffer from burnout.[9] Furthermore, practicing gratitude allows our brains to release serotonin and dopamine—two "feel good" chemicals that positively impact mood, willpower, and motivation. Over time, practicing gratitude will "train" your brain to focus on what's going well versus what isn't.

Because of our tendency to plan for all the bad stuff, gratitude is one of the most powerful antidotes to our hardwired negativity bias—that tendency to focus on negative events rather than positive ones. Further, just notice what happens to your breath when you slow down to focus on the good stuff. All the things that help us reconnect our mind and our body are so closely connected. And when you start with your shoulders, it's the present-bringing reminder that often results in a slower breathing, a more focused clear mind, and a sense that there just might be something bigger at play in this whole universe deal. And even if you don't jump on the spiritual train, gratitude often acts as a fast pass (like at Disneyland) to joy.

JOY IS A FUCKING CHOICE

Although I am becoming more of a proponent of believing you shouldn't rank emotions, that you should just feel them all and you'll be healthier because of it, I have to say that joy is my favorite. Now, it's still remarkably interesting to me that it's touted as the most vulnerable emotion on the planet.[10] Whenever I ask anybody to tell me where they feel their most vulnerable, people will use words like shame, sadness, grief, or remorse. But jumping directly to joy as something that is synonymous with vulnerability rarely happens. Vulnerability is often connected to negatively viewed emotions way quicker than it is to positive ones. When we feel an unbridled joy—just think of the last time you were belly laughing or having a shameless dance party in your kitchen—it's then that we're at our most vulnerable. That feeling and those moments are where your true soul—the center of you, that thing we were trying to get back to in the first chapter, our vulnerability—lives. Joy often occurs in short bursts and is much more intense than happy.[11] There's a depth to joy that can be considered spiritual, and I love those moments when joy moves you to tears. It tends to be the great connector, this joy thing, and a phenomenal predictor of productive work cultures and healthy family systems.[12]

Even in our most difficult moments, joy remains a choice. My friend and author Jess Janzen wrote *Bring the Joy*,[13] where she tells her story of being a mama in the front row of a funeral. And while feeling the excruciating sadness of losing a child, moments of joy were still available for the taking. Joy is indeed a choice. In our darkest days, seek and you will find—however fleeting. We need it now more than ever.

BRINGING IT BACK HOME

This second practice is all about reconnecting your head and your heart. Often when we get overwhelmed, we step out of our body and get stuck in our heads. We're still good people, even in the mess of it all. We just sometimes lose access to the best parts of us. We have the ability at any given moment to slow down our breathing and get back into the moment. If you're able to, drop your shoulders and slow your breath, even be still for a few stolen moments. Regulate your body and you have access to your words, your memories, and your capacity for kindness and compassion. For now, simply consider this: Put your hand over your heart, drop those shoulders, and breathe deep. Pause. There you are. That's what reconnection feels like. It is never an endgame. Make time for it when you're lying in bed at night reviewing all the ways you've fucked up in the day, or when you're doubting yourself the most. Anxiety and worry simply cannot exist in a calm body. When we feel like we can't control the worried thoughts and plans for all the bad stuff, simply try to drop your shoulders, relax your jaw, wiggle your toes, and breathe deep. Put it all down for a moment. You are so much more capable, competent, and powerful than you think. You will figure it out. We, together, are wired for all of it.

1. What were the times in your life, or where have you been, when you felt your most relaxed or at ease? Notice it isn't often a switch (like the day you went on vacation or the moment the project was completed). Simply removing the stressor does not remove the stress response. Pay attention to the circumstances where, or people with whom, you feel most able to put it all down for a while.

2. Start with two minutes a day of simply being still. There's no right or wrong way to do it. In fact, start with 30 seconds. Set a timer and just be still. And just notice if anything changes.

3. When you spend the majority of most days in a jacked-up body, the cortisol makes you an asshole. Give yourself a break, on purpose, as often as you're able to. And set a reminder on your phone or get your person to remind you every now and then to drop those shoulders. Do it for you and for them, too. You'll both be better for it.

CHAPTER TWELVE

Practice 3—Bringing the Bigger Picture into Focus

The Why Is in the Walking

L et's end how we started—with the answer to it all. Feeling seen is the possessed-by-all, mastered-by-none magic needed to reconnect a disconnected world. When we're in the mess of it all, this truth is what we lose access to. Staying grounded in this bigger picture is perhaps the biggest challenge, but it's the critical last practice I'll leave in your hands. Author Simon Sinek[1] first wrote about the necessity to "start with why" as the guide to keeping us grounded. I remember when I saw Simon speak in person for the first time, I was so intrigued by his clear depiction that there are two main ways to influence human behavior: manipulation and inspiration. He was clear that inspiration is the most powerful and more sustainable of the two. Indeed, you can't reward and consequence people into being calm, or kind, or great. You must show them. Being clear on that "why" is a critical practice to have in place when the road on which we're all walking home gets a little rocky. The bigger picture will always be rooted in reconnecting to the power of truly seeing each other, over and over again. When we start to understand that reconnecting this world is the thing we should all be passionate about, so much will shift.

PASSION RIDES SHOTGUN TO PURPOSE

Think about the most confident, self-assured, respected person you've spent time with in your lifetime. Someone who was passionate and inspirational. What did you notice about them? How did they treat others? How did they speak about themselves? See, when you walk with a sense of purpose, when you know where it is you're going, you show up differently. We often assume it's because they've found their passion. I think, however, that the most admirable among us are much clearer about their purpose than their passion. For me, passion rides shotgun to purpose. Passion is something that so many of us chase. We long to feel the passion that will make work feel like a joyful, meaningful, blissful endeavor. I have heard, many times, "I wish I was passionate about something"; or asked, "How do you find your passion?" I think sometimes that in our desire to find the passion, we miss being clear on the why first. Because if you can answer that question clearly—the purpose of why, as a human, you're here on this planet—it's so much easier to stay passionate about whatever it is that you do. So, I'm not looking relentlessly for this elusive passion thing. To remind me of the purpose of why I'm on this planet, I need somewhere to reconnect as frequently as I'm able. And remarkably, passion simply follows.

The question that often leads me back to this why thing the fastest is "Do you know how important you are to so many people?" "Do you know how many people love you, look up to you, are inspired by you?" And the answer profoundly for so many people is "No." I find it fascinating how much we struggle to identify just how critical we are to the people we love or even work with. One of my favorite activities to put our team through is to open the big team meetings with this question: "Why are we lucky to have you?" It's so interesting to watch people I think are amazing struggle to articulate just what they bring to the table. Furthermore, I notice how quickly other people, when they see the struggle, jump in with suggestions about what they think the team member is good at. It's a beautiful exercise.

The negativity bias comes with a strong pull. If we're not careful and conscious, we have a propensity to resort to all the things we're not. All the people we've disappointed. All the ones in our lives, at any given moment, who we assume are judging us or think poorly of us, primarily because we have a hard time recounting the times others have acknowledged us. The subsequent story in our head, fueled largely by that negativity bias, often prevents us from so much. But I can tell you this: In this moment, you have everything you need to reconnect a disconnected world. And we need you now, more than ever, to (even half-) believe that to be true. If you only knew how many are inspired by you, would love to have what you have, would love to be just like you. If we allow ourselves to practice just sitting with this truth, we would be in a place to see and be seen, maybe like never before. If you doubt this, let's flip it. Consider how often you confirm to the people in your life how much they matter to you. How often do you deliberately, on purpose, share with the people in your circle how much you admire, are inspired by, or simply notice them? Even if you're someone who can answer, "I do that all the time," I promise you, given the weight of this world, it's not nearly enough.

WHAT'S THE POINT OF IT ALL?

Passion comes easier when I remember my only job is to walk people home with everything I've got. Reminders of my why often come in quiet moments. A message from a kid I used to treat; a note tucked into my suitcase from my husband. Even when I'm away from my kids, or I feel exhausted, deflated, or worried if I've let someone down, it all becomes clearer when I ask: What is the bigger picture? How much does this matter in the grand scheme of my story here? It's the thing that is always out of focus when I struggle the most. See, we can't keep finding our passion if we don't know our purpose.

Turns out, it takes remarkably little to change the life of another. And some days we can do things that are so profoundly magical, like give blood or create a nonprofit organization for homeless teenage moms. And on other days, a smile at the kid in the subway will be all we can muster. The weight of it all seems so much more manageable when we consider this again: Your only job is to do the next, best, right, kind thing. This is truly all any of us have control over in the next moment. And it's truly all anybody needs in this world.

Respectfully sharing all your stories (and there are so many— trust me) with the world is critical—stories like ones you've read here: about Old Bill, or the dad who had supervised visits, or my "bottom hand" woman. But we often don't. I wonder if it's about not wanting to brag, or that we don't want people to know we've done kind things. But it's something I really think we should do more of. Like right now. Think about the times when you stopped to notice something. When you gave it away. You did the kind deed or the good gesture. Think about how good it felt. And I can promise you, the people you gave it away to think about you more than you know. It's the retelling of those moments that don't happen nearly enough.

I often remember my work with police officers when I think about culture and how important it is to share the "wins." One of the questions I often save for first responders is this: "Tell me about a time when you were a hero." Now, so many of them tell me that they hate the word "hero." When I've asked why, some have explained they don't like to be put on a pedestal that they may fall from; or that in the many moments they've done good things, there were so many more when they "failed." I also often think they don't always see themselves as good people because of the trauma they're living with in their heads. It took me three sessions with a police officer I'd been seeing for years to tell me about the time she might have possibly been a "hero"—when she felt *seen* in something she did that was just "part of the job."

Here's a little piece of her (edited) story. She had spent many sessions explaining to me that in her decade-long career as a police officer, she'd seen more trauma and pain than anyone could imagine, yet easily passed it off as "part of the job." She was just "numb to it all" but was easily able to recount the logistics of many calls in graphic detail. My goal was to reconnect her mind to all the emotions in her body, but I knew she had to feel not only all the negative, overwhelming, hard emotions that would flood her frequently, but to shift the narrative to the pieces of her story where she had seen another, and maybe even felt seen herself in the process.

So, when I said "Tell me about a time when you were a hero," she eventually, and reluctantly, told me these words: "You know, there was one night shift. It was just me driving around, and I saw a group of kids at this park. I went over and shone my lights in their direction. I could see they were smoking and drinking. As I stepped out of the car, kids scattered. I noticed that one of them was still there, lying on that park bench. I thought maybe he was proving a point and wasn't going to move, and quite honestly, I didn't really want to make it a big deal for him. However, of course, I walked over to make sure he was okay. As I approached, I could instantly tell this kid was in big trouble. Now, I'd worked as a paramedic for many years before I became a police officer. I knew it was against all protocol to pick him up, but I knew he didn't have much time. So, I grabbed this big kid, ran with him in my arms across the park, and then put him in the back of the police car. I drove lights and sirens to the hospital. I remember the look on the nurses' faces and the disapproval as I carried this kid through the emergency room doors. But just like me, when they took one look at him, they too knew he didn't have a lot of time. They grabbed him and immediately whisked him away. And suddenly, there I stood, empty handed, with nothing left to do but get back into my car. I finished my shift and like I've done on numerous calls before, the ones I never really talk about, I went back to check on this kid before I signed off for the night."

She continued, "I just wanted to know if this kid had made it. And so I walked back in past the nursing station. The nurse explained to me briefly that it had been touch and go throughout the night, but it appeared as though this kid was now going to make it. Through the nursing station windows, I could see his parents anxiously at his side, and I remember thinking I was glad the kid had someone there.

"And then, you know what happened?" she asked me. "I got a call the next week and it was that kid's parents. Apparently, they tracked me down from the paperwork at the hospital. And they invited me for dinner." "Did you go?" I asked her. She said, shifting in her chair, "against my better judgment, I did. I don't know why. And it was maybe one of the coolest nights of my career. To sit with his family who were so close to having buried their kid. Just in that moment, it made me realize how important my job is.

They thanked me with tears in their eyes for saving their son. And the kid was pretty neat, too."

When I asked if she had ever told that story before, maybe at the detachment or when sitting with her fellow police officers, she looked at me incredulously and said, "No! Are you kidding me? In all my years of service, I don't remember anybody reporting on the things that went well. Feels like we're bragging, and it really is truly just part of the job."

As I absorbed her words, I thought about the countless other times I'd heard people tell me they had done things they were proud of, that likely changed the lives of other people. Yet these stories had never seen the light of day. As the police officer recounted the events, I was taken aback (but not surprised) by the emotions the telling of this story (finally) summoned to her eyes. She asked me, surprised, as she teared up, "What the hell is happening here? I haven't cried in years." You see, there's power in the telling, in sharing a story and noticing the feelings it brings up when you connect it to words like "hero." We have so much power on this planet, you and me. Name it, acknowledge it, and reconnect to what matters. That is how you heal. That is how we reconnect this disconnected world.

HOW TO FIND IT

Listen. So many times I've heard people wonder if they have a passion. I think each of us is born with a life's purpose. Seeing it—creating an ideal—is a thing many talk about. I haven't ever been really clear on how I'm going to get there, but I think the most important work I've done is figuring out (and re-figuring out) where I want to be. Not long ago, I said to my personal psychologist, Jane, "I know where I'm going. There are clear (albeit audacious) goals: I would love to create a team that lives a message of reconnection that resonates with the world. I'd love school mental health programs to believe in our model of trauma-informed practice. I'd love to have a *New York Times* bestseller that will save lives, and I will speak that message on big stages with Brené, Pink, Shonda, Glennon, and Oprah." In fact, I remember giggling when I asked her, "Wouldn't it be cool to be in a place where, just like those women, people know you only by your first name? Like, a last name isn't even required?"

And you know what? She didn't even flinch. She said, "I think it's possible." What? Jesus! Did she think that was even a thing? "No, I was just kidding," I said.

"But were you?" she asked. Fuck. Maybe I wasn't. I have to tell you, her lack of flinching meant the world to me. I can remember maybe two other times, distinctly, when that happened in chasing this dream of reconnecting a disconnected world. First, Matt, the husband of Marti, my COO, once said to me, "Do you have any idea what you're building here?" I couldn't believe he believed we might be on to something. And the second time was when another one on our team, my dear Tara, said to my dad while they stood watching me on stage, "She has no idea how powerful she's about to become." My dad later told me, through tears, that hearing Tara say that made him realize he's known for years I was going to do great things, but that he was always scared to tell me. That moment meant everything.

The bigger picture will ground you. Walking your why—our why—of being the one to be seen and allowing others to feel it is truly the reason we're here. So, here are a few lessons I've learned about walking that why, that purpose, to keep us all in the game. I'd love to leave them with you, so maybe we can continue to do this together. Truly, all we need are you and me.

LESSON ONE: CALL YOUR SHOT
AND FIND YOUR PEOPLE

Find a safe place (even if it's in your own journal) to put out into the world the biggest of big dreams. Like the boldest, most important thing you think you were born to do. And then find people—even just one or two—who believe it's possible. As lawyer and author Daniel Pink[2] has resoundingly concluded, what people regret most in life, particularly as they age, are the things they didn't do, not the things they did. Our biggest regrets tend to involve our lack of boldness—we didn't ask them out, we didn't speak up, we didn't take that job abroad. Missing opportunities to be kind or give grace—those are the things we wish we had done. Regrets are not bad things—they are sometimes our greatest teachers. This is so connected to vulnerability, courage, and going all in. Giving people the permission and safety (not looking away during the audacious dreams) to be appropriately bold is one of the most important shifts I think you and I can do for ourselves and for the people we love. Saying, out loud, that I will speak on the big stages, maybe write a bestseller, feels silly, especially if those things don't come to fruition. But I promise you, you have to call your shot. And the bigger the better. Someone who won't flinch needs to hear it. When my psychologist Jane didn't doubt my big dreams, when this team wanted me to win sometimes even more that I did, it was clear that I couldn't do it on self-resolve alone. Call your shot and find your people.

LESSON TWO: UNDERESTIMATE ME

This one, I can imagine, won't be for everyone. But I have to tell you, this one's my biggest motivator. It's cliché when we hear people say you shouldn't play to the haters. Don't worry about what people think. Although I believe that to be true, it's so much easier said than done. I have spent a lot of energy worrying about what one person thinks, sometimes at the expense of so many more who are in my corner. It is easy to be derailed by one negative opinion or comment. I don't think that worry ever goes away.

My approach has been to flip it. And instead of trying to avoid the negative criticism or the ones who don't seem to understand your intention, welcome them in and use that doubt as fuel. Picture the people who have underestimated you the most. And then prove them wrong. One small step at a time. I think it might be my favorite thing—to be underestimated. "Jody, you'll never survive in this industry if you continue to swear." I'll take my chances. Authenticity is not a compromise. "Jody, a book? You're not a writer." Then I'll just write what I have to say. And now we have a book deal with HarperCollins. "Running a multimillion-dollar company? As a woman? With no business experience?" Watch me. And when I don't know what I'm doing, I'll find the people who do. When you sit with those winners, those conversations are different, and I am always better for it. "Stay away from the controversial conversations—you want to play it safe." Sorry—doesn't align with the values. We're here for the hard conversations—and we know we'll fuck them up. And that's okay. Even when we lose relationships along the way.

The goal is to continue to rack up these underestimations. And kindly crush them. I chase this daily.

LESSON THREE: SERVE THE MESSAGE

This is the most important. Pick a value or even just a word that is uncompromisable to your person, your brand, or your practice. What aligns with who you want to be or what you want to be remembered for? Around here, we change the list and often add to it, but I want you to think about what might fit for you. What would you fight to be known for? Here are the words our team lives by: brave, audacious, inclusive, kind, authentic, and relentless. Every time we're faced with a big decision, it's a simple question: Does it serve the message? Does the decision we're about to make, the stance we're about to take, the people we're aligning ourselves with . . . does it serve the message and fit our values? If the answer is no, then it, whatever it is, no matter how shiny it appears, is also a no.

Eyes on the horizon with a clear, relentless, uncompromising resolve. I think that should always be the plan. The problem with us, mostly, is that we want to get there yesterday. Patience—I fucking hate that word—is a virtue, apparently. And here's also the deal with big goals, big dreams, and audacious "whys." Even if you don't arrive at the big goals, you don't win the gold medal, you don't get the *New York Times* bestseller—when you're going all in, your purpose on this planet will present itself. Sometimes the things we find along the way to the big thing matter way more than getting there.

COMING FULL CIRCLE

I'm clear that I want to create, and be a part of, a safe space for anyone and everyone to land as we harness the power required to walk each other home. This goal takes courage. As psychologist Susan David says, "Courage is not the absence of fear. Courage is fear, walking."[3] Walking your why is sometimes about moving toward the thing that you'd rather not do—living your values even at the cost of losing a big relationship or an opportunity. Walking it—for me—means that every day I, we, have the power not only to change a life, but in this climate of disconnect, divisiveness, and subsequent havoc that is unleashed on our emotional well-being, to know that our power of reconnection can save a life. That awareness of just how much this world needs a simple act of connection gets me out of bed every single morning, with a vengeance.

At the core, we are all good people. I have to believe that to be true. What happens to us defines how we layer our armor. In my mind, I picture the most hurtful or traumatizing experiences as the layers that are the most impenetrable. Although they were developed to protect a tender soul, they are the hardest to break through when it's safe enough to heal. Those of us with fewer "layers," or those who have been lucky (privileged?) enough to be surrounded by people who can connect and reconnect in healthy ways, make that armor less necessary. See, it's only in a relationship that those who walk among us will be brave enough to pull back the layers. And when we are brave enough to remember that we can facilitate that in each other (no matter how small of an effort we are able to take), we will create significant, impactful change in the short time we're here. That, my friends, on my clearest day, is our collective purpose.

Often, truly seeing another happens in the most unexpected places. I received a particularly important lesson at the hockey rink, from an amazing fellow hockey mom. As exasperated as our own children can make us, there is an indescribable joy that can be found in the woes of parenting. I can also tell you that being reminded your kids are watching how you handle things can put a significant amount of conflicting pressure on stepping up to walk your why. That responsibility to do right by your children, many have said, has kept them going in the best of times and even kept them alive in the worst moments. Here's a hard little chapter for Asher and me.

I knew the second I walked into that hockey dressing room that this was not a place for moms. I had brought Asher a Gatorade between try-out periods, and the room, filled with preteen and teen boys, fell silent. I handed Asher the drink (but I kept the candy bag in my jacket because that would have been super uncool) and turned to go. Then I heard him say, loudly, "Hey mama!" (Cringe! Jesus, kid. Probably don't say "mama" in a room full of teenage boys.) I said, "Yes?" He said, "See that kid there," pointing across the room at a big dude, red faced and sweaty. "I tried to sit by him to get dressed today and he told me he'd break my fucking shins if I sat near him." All eyes. On me. I said, "Cool" (seriously). I looked at the red-faced kid, who dropped his head. The two junior hockey players walking these kids through try-out practice did the same. I felt myself backing toward the door. A sense of trying to be the cool kid in my own awkward days washed over me as I tried to find just the right words to not embarrass Asher or the red-faced kid, but be the cool mom who drops it like it's hot. This is what I came up with: "Well, I guess it's a good thing you didn't sit by him then." Followed way too quickly by, "Okay then, team. Have a great next game out there, eh?" What. The. Fuck. As I ran up the steps from the dressing room, I went directly to Aaron to tell him that our kid was likely fixing to get the shit beat out of him. His comment? "Why did you go down there?" Not helpful.

Fast-forward to after-practice the next night. Asher was in tears. He's going to quit hockey. The stories of despair and being bullied on the ice came fast and furious. The red-faced dude took his place on the bench and made fun of him. Apparently, he talked about him like he wasn't there, wondering why Asher was such a "mama suck."

What do you do when it's your kid? I contemplated for hours. Aaron suggested that Asher meet the kid at the bike rack at school. My mom's suggestion was to tell Asher to "punch him." Sweet Jesus. And all I was hoping for was this stupid shit I talked about all the time—some empathy for this 13-year-old-boy who was just trying to do his best to fit in, too. I knew I needed to call his mom. Or do I just let it lose steam? We'll all forget about it next week, right? Even as I write these words, I still feel like that was one of the biggest decisions in my whole life. (How do people *do* this parenting thing? And why do I feel so incompetent?) I asked Marti if she would call this kid's mom, and she said, "Fuck, no. But I'm not like you, Jod. This is the best move. I just don't know if I'd be brave enough to do it."

So, you know what? I looked up the mom's number on the team app and I texted a little note and hit Send before I could rethink it. I said something like, "Hi. It's Jody Carrington here. Our boys are on the same try-out team. Asher came home talking about the practice last night and I just want to make sure my kid wasn't being a jerk to yours. If you get a few free minutes today, anytime, could you give me a quick call?"

Just when I started to breathe again, the phone rang. She didn't even say "Hi." She said, "Just got your text. Is that code for my kid was being a dick to your kid?"

Oh, dear. Here we go. And then we talked, and I told her what I knew—including the "break your fucking shins" part. And I instantly felt terrible. She said, "I can't imagine him speaking like that, I really can't. But you can be sure I will talk to him tonight."

We exchanged pleasantries, I thanked her, and I hung up. I felt like shit for a few hours, to be honest. When I got home, Asher asked me even before my coat was off, "Mom, did you talk to his mom?" And then I knew that it was an important risk. I had to show him that the hard conversations were worth it, regardless of outcome. I told him she was so great, we talked, and that I wasn't sure what was going to happen. But what's important to me is that when hard things happen, I'm so glad you tell me (even if it's in front of a team of teenagers!).

We didn't hear anything back. Seriously, it was interesting to feel the shift in knowing that a conversation was had, I was kind and so was she, and Asher knew I did it. And then the following morning, I read these words. And cried. (I give them to you verbatim because I think it's important. I just changed the name of the kid.)

Good morning, Jody,

Thank you again for chatting with me yesterday and bringing to light what was going on with Jesse and Asher in the dressing room. Obviously not the news I want to hear but I'm very thankful I get this chance to get Jesse to realize how horrible his behavior was . . . and learn from it!

I do regret that I did not get back to you and Asher by last night! My day yesterday did not give me many opportunities to have a proper and meaningful chat with Jesse until later on. I hope this delay didn't upset Asher or yourself. Today, Jesse says he is going to apologize to Asher in the dressing room, or perhaps whenever he sees him first. This morning he sat down and wrote a note to Asher. Please understand this note isn't just some sort of "checking the box" type of action for us. These days have me growing a bit more skeptical than usual so that might be my first assumption if I were in your shoes. He wrote it himself this morning after breakfast. I suggested the idea as I've learned in my house full of males how expressing their apologies is often nothing more than a quiet mumble . . . My husband and I take this very seriously and I do believe Jesse has sincerely realized his actions were hurtful and wrong, to say the least. He often tries to be the funny guy with his friends and brothers . . . but he's well aware now that his actions with Asher made him a complete bully and nothing else!

I'll be dropping Jesse off at the rink with his hockey gear and his letter for Asher. I am hoping his emotions don't get the best of him and it goes well. I shall check in with you later . . .

Can I just tell you that, as I read every word, my heart swelled and I fell more in love with this mama? Just like me, doing the best she can. And she didn't look away. Two days after this note, we met up face to face in the hockey rink. She is as lovely in person. We see each other every now and then. My respect for her is enormous. And the part I loved most? When we left that first face-to-face meeting, she said, "I wish I would have done this for our oldest when he came home in tears from the hockey rink and never went back. This was an important conversation." Oh, dear mama, if you only knew. You gave me so much more with your words and your kindness. You showed me how to do it. This walking each other home is often painful, but oh how beautiful it can be. Feeling seen makes this journey so much more manageable.

BRINGING IT BACK HOME—ONE LAST TIME

This final of the big three is perhaps the ultimate in the grounding forces. Even when I feel disconnected from my people and when I don't have any damn time to slow down and just breathe, I am often fueled most by a clarity around just how much I matter in this moment. I usually have much more access to that "why" when I have the first two practices on board—when I am reconnected to my people, and I am remembering to breathe. But the first two aren't necessary to step fully into this practice. In fact, sometimes when I'm struggling to make sense of why everyone is an asshole and I can't slow down long enough to find the empathy, I am reminded of why I'm here: to do the next, best, right, kind thing in this human race. We're all headed to the same place. None of us knows for sure just how many heartbeats we have left. Not missing the moments matters even more than getting it just right. It seems we might not always know how to get there, but having our sights set on the horizon, even if there's a huge tangled mess with winding roads and dead ends in the middle, can give us all the power we need to remember that we are so important in this bigger plan. We matter so much to so many. If you only knew. And now, at least in this moment, I hope you do.

I'll leave you, once again, with a few of the words we started with from Richard Wagamese:

From the moment we are born to the time we continue on our spirit journey, we are involved in the creation of the story of our time here. It is what we arrive with. It is all we leave behind.

Share your story so others can see themselves in yours. And write a good one, dear friend. It's been an honor to sit with you. Here's to reconnecting in all your chapters to come.

ACKNOWLEDGMENTS

I wish to thank the readers of early drafts, who so graciously gave me their time, their insights, and their blessings. I am forever grateful to Sarah Adomako-Ansah, Rebecca Martini, Clarissa Chambers, Cam Foss, Dan Liebman, Patti Liogier, Jeff Lohnes, Chau Lui, Laurie McIntosh, Dr. Milena Radzikowska, Michele Ranger, Linda Sivertsen, Dr. Scharie Tavcer, and Brad Wilson.

To the people whose (edited) stories I told: Pieces of your stories shaped mine and this work. It was a privilege and an honor to be a part of your chapters.

NOTES

Introduction

1. Caine, V., Murphy, M. S., Estefan, A., Clandinin, D. J., Steeves, P., & Huber, J. (2016). Exploring the purposes of fictionalization in narrative inquiry. *Qualitative Inquiry*, 23(3).

PART ONE: HOW WE GOT SO LOST

1. Summit LA18. Esther Perel: The quality of your relationships determines the quality of your life. YouTube. (2019, February 12). https://www.youtube.com/watch?v=LmDPAOE5V2Y

2. Dass, R., & Bush, M. (2018). *Walking each other home* [Audiobook]. Sounds True.

3. van der Kolk, B. (2014). *The body keeps the score: Brain, mind, and body in the healing of trauma*. Penguin Books.

4. Siegel, D. (2016, July 10). Dr. Dan Siegel: If you can name it, you can tame it. *Keeping in Touch BC*. https://www.keepingintouchbc.com/blog/2016/07/11/dr-dan-siegel-can-name-can-tame

Chapter One: Emotional Dysregulation

1. Siegel, D. J., & Bryson, T. P. (2019). *The yes brain: How to cultivate courage, curiosity, and resilience in your child*. Bantam.

2. Katz, C., Tsur, N., Talmon, A., & Nicolet, R. (2021). Beyond fight, flight, and freeze: Towards a new conceptualization of peritraumatic responses

to child sexual abuse based on retrospective accounts of adult survivors. *Child Abuse & Neglect*, 112. https://doi.org/10.1016/j.chiabu.2020.104905

3. Li, P. (2021, December 25). Emotional regulation in children: A complete guide. https://www.parentingforbrain.com/self-regulation-toddler-temper-tantrums

4. Brandt, K., Perry, B. D., Seligman, S., & Tronick, E. (2013). Infant and early childhood mental health: Core concepts and clinical practice. American Psychiatric Association Publishing.

5. Watson, J. B. (1913). Psychology as the behaviorist views it. *Psychological Review*, 20(2), 158–177.

6. Skinner B. F. (1953). *Science and human behavior*. Macmillan.

7. Pavlov, I. P. (2003). *Conditioned reflexes*. Dover Publications.

8. Robinson, D. (1995). *An intellectual history of psychology*. University of Wisconsin Press.

9. Brown, B. (2021). *Atlas of the heart: Mapping meaningful connection and the language of human experience*. Random House.

10. Buehler, E. D. (2021). State and local law enforcement training academies, 2018 – statistical tables. *Bureau of Justice Statistics*. https://bjs.ojp.gov/sites/g/files/xyckuh236/files/media/document/slleta18st.pdf

11. Conti, N. (2011). Weak links and warrior hearts: A framework for judging self and others in police training. *Police Practice and Research*, 12(5), 410–423.

12. Goss, K., & Allan, S. (2009). Shame, pride, and eating disorders. *Clinical Psychology & Psychotherapy*, 6(4), 303–316.

13. Brown, B. (2021). *Atlas of the heart: Mapping meaningful connection and the language of human experience*. Random House.

CHAPTER TWO: NO WORDS

1. Pittman, R. (2021). How to talk with kids about healthy relationships. https://www.poehealth.org/how-to-talk-with-kids-about-healthy-relationships

2. Brown, B. (2021). *Atlas of the heart: Mapping meaningful connection and the language of human experience*. Random House.

3. Pratt, L. A., Druss, B. G., Manderscheid, R. W., & Walker, E. R. (2016).

Excess mortality due to depression and anxiety in the United States: Results from a nationally representative survey. *General Hospital Psychiatry*, 39, 39–45.

4. Barrett, L. F. (2018). *How emotions are made: The secret life of the brain*. Harper Paperbacks.

5. Arden, J. B. (2010). *Rewire your brain: Think your way to a better life*. John Wiley & Sons.

6. Barrett, L. F. (2018). *How emotions are made: The secret life of the brain*. Harper Paperbacks.

7. Hillig, C. (2007). *Seeds for the soul: Living as the source of who you are*. Sentient Publications.

8. Goleman, D. (2005). *Emotional intelligence: Why it can matter more than IQ*. Bantam.

9. Ahanger, R. G. (2012). Emotional intelligence: The most potent factor of job performance among executives. In A. Di Fabio (Ed.), *Emotional intelligence: New perspectives and applications*. Intechopen.

10. Stadthagen-González, H., Ferré, P., Pérez-Sánchez, M. A., Imbault, C., & Hinojosa, J. A. (2018). Norms for 10,491 Spanish words for five discrete emotions: Happiness, disgust, anger, fear, and sadness. *Behavior Research Methods* 50(5):1943–1952.

11. Kwon, D. (2019, December 19). Emotional words such as "love" mean different things in different languages. https://www.scientificamerican .com/article/emotional-words-such-as-love-mean-different-things-in -different-languages

12. Nangyeon, L. (2016). Cultural differences in emotion: Differences in emotional arousal level between the East and the West. *Integrative Medicine Research*, 5(2), 105–109.

13. Brown, N., McIlwraith, T., & Tubelle de González, L. (2020). *Perspectives: An open introduction to cultural anthropology* (2nd ed.). American Anthropological Association. https://perspectives.americananthro.org/ Chapters/Perspectives.pdf

14. David, S. (2016). *Emotional agility: Get unstuck, embrace change, and thrive in work and life*. Penguin Random House.

15. Schwartz, R. (2021). *No bad parts: Healing trauma and restoring wholeness with the internal family systems model.* Sounds True.

16. Mithlo, N. M. (2011). Blood memory and the arts: Indigenous genealogies and imagined truths. *American Indian Culture and Research Journal, 35*(4), 103–118.

17. Atlas, G. (2022). *Emotional inheritance: A therapist, her patients, and the legacy of trauma.* Little, Brown Spark.

18. Neufeld, G., & Maté, G. (2013). *Hold onto your kids: Why parents need to matter more than peers.* Knopf Canada.

19. Thistle, J. (2019). *From the ashes: My story of being Métis, homeless, and finding my way back.* Simon & Schuster Canada.

20. Kahneman, D., & Deaton, A. (2010). High income improves evaluation of life but not emotional well-being. *Proceedings of the National Academy of Sciences, 107*(38), 16489–16493.

21. Seligman, M. E. P. (2006). *Learned optimism: How to change your mind and your life.* Vintage.

22. To see more by Shawn Achor, visit https://www.shawnachor.com/happiness-advantage-key-takeaways

23. Lyubomirsky, S., & King, L. (2005). The benefits of frequent positive affect: Does happiness lead to success? *Psychological Bulletin, 131*(6), 803–855.

24. Achor, S. (2010). *The happiness advantage: How a positive brain fuels success in work and life.* GoodThink Inc.

25. Berinato, S. (2020). That discomfort you're feeling is grief. https://hbr.org/2020/03/that-discomfort-youre-feeling-is-grief

26. Wolfelt, A. D. (2021). *Understanding your grief: Ten essential touchstones for finding hope and healing your heart* (2nd ed.). Companion Press.

27. O'Connor, M. F. (2019). Grief: A brief history of research on how body, mind, and brain adapt. *Psychosomatic Medicine, 81*(8): 731–738.

28. Palmer, P. J. (2016). The gift of presence, the perils of advice. On Being Project (2021). https://onbeing.org/blog/the-gift-of-presence-the-perils-of-advice/.

29. Ormel, J., Kessler, R. C., & Schoevers, R. (2019). Depression: more treatment but no drop in prevalence—How effective is treatment? And can we do better? *Current Opinion in Psychiatry, 32*(4), 348–354.

30. Neimeyer, R. A., & Currier, J. M. (2009). Grief therapy: Evidence of efficacy and emerging directions. *Current Directions in Psychological Science,* 18(6), 352–356.

31. Kessler, D. (2019). *Finding meaning: The sixth stage of grief.* Scribner.

32. Kübler-Ross, E., (1969). *On death and dying.* Scribner.

33. Kessler, D. (2019). *Finding meaning: The sixth stage of grief.* Scribner.

34. Ackerman, C. E. (2021, December 13). What is gratitude and why is it so important? https://positivepsychology.com/gratitude-appreciation

35. Doyle, G. (2020). *Untamed.* Penguin Random House.

CHAPTER THREE: THAT RELATIONSHIP THING

1. Pinker, S. (2015). *The village effect: How face-to-face contact can make us healthier and happier.* Penguin Random House.

2. Baer, D. (2015, November 12). A psychologist visited an Italian island to find out why so many people lived to 100—and discovered something amazing. https://www.businessinsider.com/susan-pinker-discovered-why-so-many-sardinians-live-to-100-2015-11

3. Craigie, T. A., Brooks-Gunn, J., & Waldfogel, J. (2012). Family structure, family stability and outcomes of five-year-old children. *Families, Relationships and Societies,* 1(1), 43–61.

4. Carrington, J. (2019). *Kids these days: A game plan for (re)connection to those we teach, lead, and love.* Impress.

5. Gibran, K. (1923). "On Children." *The prophet.* Knopf. https://poets.org/poem/children-1

6. Wang, W., & Parker, K. (2014). Record share of Americans have never married. Pew Research Center. https://www.pewresearch.org/social-trends/2014/09/24/record-share-of-americans-have-never-married

7. Bowlby, J. (1997). *Attachment and Loss:* Vol. 1, *Attachment.* Pimlico.

8. Watson, J. C., & Greenberg, L. S. (2017). Emotion-focused therapy for generalized anxiety. American Psychological Association.

9. EFT Resource Center. What is EFT? http://www.eftresourcecenter.com/emotionally-focused-therapy-eft

10. Gottman, J. M. (2000). *The seven principles for making marriage work: A practical guide from the country's foremost relationship expert.* Harmony.

11. Chapman, G. (2015). *The 5 love languages: The secret to love that lasts.* Northfield.

12. Lerner, H. (2017). *Why won't you apologize?: Healing big betrayals and everyday hurts.* Gallery Books.

13. Pflug, M. C. (2017, June 4). Using the word "but": A brief guide to sincerity & clarity. https://medium.com/@mcpflugie/using-the-word-but-a-brief-guide-to-sincerity-clarity-ab311a2af6a6

14. Chapman, G. D., & Thomas, J.M. (2008). *The five languages of apology: How to experience healing in all your relationships.* Northfield.

CHAPTER FOUR: TRAUMA

1. Thompson, K. L., Hannan, S. M., & Miron, L. R. (2014). Fight, flight, and freeze: Threat sensitivity and emotion dysregulation in survivors of chronic childhood maltreatment. *Personality and Individual Differences, 69,* 28–32.

2. van der Kolk, B. (2015). *The body keeps the score: Brain, mind, and body in the healing of trauma.* Penguin Books.

3. Perel, E. (2017). *The state of affairs: Rethinking infidelity.* Harper.

4. Worthman, C. M. (2019). Shared and local pathways in suffering and resilience: Keeping the body in mind. *Transcultural Psychiatry, 56*(4), 775–785.

5. Statista. (2022). Number of divorced people in Canada in 2021, by age group. https://www.statista.com/statistics/446186/divorced-people-in-canada-by-age-group

6. Conroy, S. (2019). Family violence in Canada: A statistical profile, 2019. Canadian Centre for Justice and Community Safety Statistics. https://www150.statcan.gc.ca/n1/pub/85-002-x/2021001/article/00001/03-eng.htm

7. St. Denis, V., & Schick, C. (2003). What makes anti-racist pedagogy in teacher education difficult? Three popular ideological assumptions. *Alberta Journal of Educational Research, 49*(1). https://doi.org/10.11575/ajer.v49i1.54959

8. Moreland-Capuia, A. (2021). *The trauma of racism: Exploring the systems and people fear built.* Springer Books.

9. Justice Canada (2021, July 7). About family violence. https://www.justice
    .gc.ca/eng/cj-jp/fv-vf/about-apropos.html

10. van der Kolk, B. (2015). *The body keeps the score: Brain, mind, and body in the
    healing of trauma.* Penguin Books.

11. Mann, D. (2021, October 8). Study confirms rise in child abuse during
    COVID pandemic. HealthDay. https://consumer.healthday.com/10-8-
    study-confirms-rise-in-child-abuse-during-covid-pandemic-2655219497.html

12. World Health Organization (2020). Child maltreatment and alcohol.
    https://www.who.int/violence_injury_prevention/violence/world
    _report/factsheets/fs_child.pdf

13. Felitti, V. J., Anda, R. F., Nordenberg, D., Williamson, D. F., Spitz, A. M.,
    Edwards, V., Koss, M. P., & Marks, J. S. (1998). Relationship of childhood
    abuse and household dysfunction to many of the leading causes of death
    in adults. The Adverse Childhood Experiences (ACE) Study. *American
    Journal of Preventive Medicine,* 14(4), 245–258.

14. DeNoon, D. J. (2012, February 1). In dollars alone, cost of U.S. child abuse
    high. https://www.webmd.com/children/news/20120201/in-dollars-alone
    -cost-of-us-child-abuse-high

15. Conroy, S. Canadian Centre for Justice and Community Safety Statistics
    (2021, March 2). Family violence in Canada: A statistical profile, 2019.
    https://www150.statcan.gc.ca/n1/pub/85-002-x/2021001/article/
    00001-eng.htm

16. Cotter, Adam, Canadian Centre for Justice and Community Safety Statistics
    (2021, April 26). Intimate partner violence in Canada, 2018: An overview.
    https://www150.statcan.gc.ca/n1/pub/85-002-x/2021001/article/00003
    -eng.htm

17. World Health Organization (2020, March 26). COVID-19 and violence
    against women: What the health sector/system can do. https://www
    .who.int/reproductivehealth/publications/emergencies/COVID-19-VAW
    -full-text.pdf

18. Senate of Canada (2019). Sexual harassment and violence in the Canadian
    Armed Forces. https://sencanada.ca/content/sen/committee/421/
    SECD/Reports/SECD_Report_harassment_May_19_e.pdf

19. CBC News (2021, June 4). Your questions answered about Canada's residential school system. https://www.cbc.ca/news/canada/canada-residential-schools-kamloops-faq-1.6051632

20. Kirby, J. (2018, May 16). The sex abuse scandal surrounding USA gymnastics team doctor Larry Nassar, explained. https://www.vox.com/identities2018/1/19/16897722/sexual-abuse-usa-gymnastics-larry-nassar-explained

21. National Public Radio (2021, October 28). Former NHL player sues Blackhawks and speaks out about sexual abuse. https://www.npr.org/2021/10/28/1049923904/former-nhl-player-sues-blackhawks-and-speaks-out-about-sexual-abuse

22. Gatehouse, J., McNair, M., Angelovski, I., & Zakreski, D. (2021, May 7). Former player details alleged sexual assault by junior hockey coach Bernie Lynch. *CBC News*. https://www.cbc.ca/news/canada/bernie-lynch-junior-hockey-sexual-assault-allegation-1.6016366

23. Stamarski, C. S., & Son Hing, L. S. (2015). Gender inequalities in the workplace: The effects of organizational structures, processes, practices, and decision makers' sexism. *Frontiers in Psychology, 6*, 1400.

24. Bremner, J. D. (2006). Traumatic stress: Effects on the brain. *Dialogues in Clinical Neuroscience, 8*(4), 445–461.

25. Abend, R., Gold, A. L., Britton, J. C., Michalska, K. J., Shechner, T., Sachs, J. F., Winkler, A. M., Leibenluft, E., Averbeck, B. B., & Pine, D. S. (2020). Anticipatory threat responding: Associations with anxiety, development, and brain structure. *Biological Psychiatry, 87*(10), 916–925.

26. Wei-May, S., & Stone, L. (2020). Adult survivors of childhood trauma: Complex trauma, complex needs. *Australian Journal of General Practice, 49*(7), 423–430.

27. American Psychological Association (2020). *APA Dictionary of Psychology.* https://dictionary.apa.org/infidelity

28. Labrecque, L. T., & Whisman, M. A. (2020). Extramarital sex and marital dissolution: Does identity of the extramarital partner matter? *Family Process, 59*(3), 1308–1318.

29. Cuomo, C. (2017, December). Rethinking infidelity with Esther Perel. Purist. https://thepuristonline.com/2017/12/rethinking-infidelity-with-esther-perel/

30. Fye, M. A., & Mims, G. A. (2019). Preventing infidelity: A theory of protective factors. *The Family Journal, 27*(1), 22–30.

31. Vangelisti, A. L., & Gerstenberger, M. (2004). Communication and marital infidelity. In J. Duncombe, K. Harrison, G. Allan, & D. Marsden (Eds.), *The state of affairs* (1st ed., pp. 59–78). Routledge.

32. Page, R. E. (2012). *Stories and social media: Identities and interaction.* Routledge.

33. Wróblewska-Skrzek, J. (2021). Infidelity in relation to sex and gender: The perspective of sociobiology versus the perspective of sociology of emotions. *Sexuality & Culture, 25,* 1885–1894.

34. Doyle, G. (2020). *Untamed.* Penguin Random House.

35. Luscombe, B. (2018). The divorce rate is dropping. That may not actually be good news. *Time News.* https://time.com/5434949/divorce-rate-children-marriage-benefits

36. Huston, M. (2012, February 6). The high failure rate of second and third marriages. https://www.psychologytoday.com/ca/blog/the-intelligent-divorce/201202/the-high-failure-rate-of-second-and-third-marriages

37. McDermott, R., Fowler, J. H., & Christakis, N. A. (2013). Breaking up is hard to do, unless everyone else is doing it too: Network effects on divorce in a longitudinal sample. *Social Forces, 92*(2), 491–519.

Chapter Five: The Weight of Our Workplaces

1. International Labour Organization (2018, March). The gender gap in employment: What's holding women back? https://www.ilo.org/infostories/en-GB/Stories/Employment/barriers-women#intro

2. Clear, J. (2018). *Atomic habits: An easy and proven way to build good habits and break bad ones.* Penguin Random House.

3. Greenwood, K., & Anas, J. (2021, October 4). It's a new era for mental health at work. *Harvard Business Review.* https://hbr.org/2021/10/its-a-new-era-for-mental-health-at-work

4. Freudenberger, H. J. (1974). Staff burn-out. *Journal of Sociological Issues, 30*, 159–165.

5. Garton, E. (2017, April 6). Employee burnout is a problem with the company, not the person. *Harvard Business Review*. https://hbr.org/2017/04/employee-burnout-is-a-problem-with-the-company-not-the-person.

6. Government of Canada (2016, July 14). Psychological health in the workplace. https://www.canada.ca/en/employment-social-development/services/health-safety/reports/psychological-health.html

7. Greenwood, K., Bapat, V., & Maughan, M. (2019, November 22). Research: People want their employers to talk about mental health. https://hbr.org/2019/10/research-people-want-their-employers-to-talk-about-mental-health

8. Schaufeli, W. (2021). The burnout enigma solved? *Scandinavian Journal of Work, Environment & Health, 47*(3), 169–170.

9. Figley, C. R. (1995). Compassion fatigue: Toward a new understanding of the costs of caring. In B. H. Stamm (Ed.), *Secondary traumatic stress: Self-care issues for clinicians, researchers, and educators* (pp. 3–28). The Sidran Press.

10. Maté, G., & Maté, D. (2022). *The myth of normal: Trauma, illness, and healing in a toxic culture.* Knopf Canada.

11. De Neve, J-E., & Ward, G. (2017). Happiness at work. World Happiness Report 2017. https://s3.amazonaws.com/happiness-report/2017 HR17-Ch6_wAppendix.pdf

12. Bikos, L. J. (2020). It's all window dressing: Canadian police officers' perceptions of mental health stigma in their workplace. *Policing: An International Journal, 44*(1), 63–76.

13. Velazquez, E., & Hernandez, M. (2019). Effects of police officer exposure to traumatic experiences and recognizing the stigma associated with police officer mental health: A state-of-the-art review. *Policing: An International Journal, 42*(4), 711–724.

14. Boateng, F. D., Hsieh, M.-L., & Pryce, D. K. (2021). Police criminality: Nature and extent of crimes committed by female police officers. *Police Quarterly.* https://doi.org/10.1177/10986111211044070

15. Stinson, P. M., & Liederbach, J. (2013). Fox in the henhouse: A study of police officers arrested for crimes associated with domestic and/or family violence. *Criminal Justice Policy Review*, 24(5), 601–625.

16. Stinson, P. M., Liederbach, J., Brewer, S. L., & Mathna, B. E. (2015). Police sexual misconduct: A national scale study of arrested officers. *Criminal Justice Policy Review*, 26(7), 665–690.

17. Carleton, R. N., Afifi, T. O., Turner, S., Taillieu, T., LeBouthiller, D. M., Duranceau, S., Sareen, J., Ricciardelli, R., MacPhee, R. S., Krakauer, R., Anderson, G. S., Cramm, H. A., Groll, D., & McCreary, D. R. (2018). Exposures to potentially traumatic events among public safety personnel in Canada. *Canadian Journal of Behavioural Science*, 51(1), 37–52.

18. Mausz, J., Johnston, M., & Donnelly, E. A. (2021). The role of organizational culture in normalizing paramedic exposure to violence. *Journal of Aggression, Conflict, & Peace Research*. https://doi.org/10.1108/JACPR-06-2021-0607

19. Edwards, F., Hedwig, L., & Esposito, M. (2019). Risk of being killed by police use of force in the United States by age, race-ethnicity, and sex. *Proceedings of the National Academy of Sciences*, 116, 16793–16798.

20. Lavoie, J. G., Kaufert, J. M., Browne, A. J., Mah, S., & O'Neil, J. D. (2015). Negotiating barriers, navigating the maze: First Nations peoples' experience of medical relocation. *Canadian Public Administration*, 58(2).

21. Collins, P. (2019, April 8). Psychological debriefing—are we doing more harm than good? https://www.blueline.ca/psychological-debriefing-are-we-doing-more-harm-than-good-6321

22. Nagoski, E., & Nagoski, A. (2020). *Burnout: The secret to unlocking the stress cycle*. Ballantine Books.

CHAPTER SIX: THE DAWN OF DISCONNECT

1. Abernethy, D. B. (2002). *The dynamics of global dominance: European overseas empires, 1415–1980*. Yale University Press.

2. Rodriguez, D. (2017). White supremacy. In *The Wiley Blackwell Encyclopedia of Social Theory*. https://doi-org.libproxy.mtroyal.ca/10.1002/9781118430873.esto407

3. Marshall, T., & Gallant, D. (2021, June 1). Residential schools in Canada. https://www.thecanadianencyclopedia.ca/en/article/residential-schools

4. Austen, I., & Bilefsky, D. (2021, July 30). Hundreds more unmarked graves found at former residential school in Canada. https://www.nytimes.com /2021/06/24/world/canada/indigenous-children-graves-saskatchewan -canada.html

5. Hamilton, S. (2015). Where are the children buried? National Centre for Truth and Reconciliation, University of Manitoba. https://ehprnh2mw03 .exactdn.com/wp-content/uploads/2021/05/AAAA-Hamilton-Report -Illustrations-final.pdf

6. Aziz, S. (2021, September 30). 1st National Day for Truth and Reconciliation draws mixed feelings from Indigenous community. Global News. https:// globalnews.ca/news/8229228/national-day-truth-reconcilitation-sept-30 -indigenous/#:~:text=In%20total%2C%20as%20of%20June,the%20 British%20Columbia%20Treaty%20Commission

7. Bell, A. C., Burkley, M., & Bock, J. (2019). Examining the asymmetry in judgments of racism in self and others. *Journal of Social Psychology*, 159(5), 611–627.

8. Bagalini, A. (2020, September 26). 3 cognitive biases perpetuating racism at work—and how to overcome them. The Big Think. https://bigthink .com/the-present/cognitive-bias-racism-at-work

9. Hall, W. J., Chapman, M. V., Lee, K. M., Merino, Y. M., Thomas, T. W., Payne, B. K., Eng, E., Day, S. H., & Coyne-Beasley, T. (2015). Implicit racial/ethnic bias among health care professionals and its influence on health care outcomes: A systematic review. *American Journal of Public Health*, 105(12), e60–e76. https://doi.org/10.2105/AJPH.2015.302903

10. García, J. D. (2018). *Privilege (Social Inequality)*. Salem Press Encyclopedia.

11. National Center for Drug Abuse Statistics (2022). Drug abuse statistics. https://drugabusestatistics.org/#:~:text=Substance%20Abuse%20 Statistics,drugs%20within%20the%20last%20year

12. Sun, Y., Li, Y., Bao, Y., Meng, S., Sun, Y., Schumann, G., Kosten, T., Strang, J., Lu, L., & Shi, J. (2020). Brief report: Increased addictive internet and substance use behavior during the COVID-19 pandemic in China. *American Journal on Addictions*, 29(4), 268–270.

13. Hari, J. (2015, January 27). Can connection cure addiction? *Greater Good Magazine.* https://greatergood.berkeley.edu/article/item/can_connection _cure_addiction

14. Fleming, A. (2019, January 9). Constant cravings: Is addiction on the rise? *The Guardian.* https://www.theguardian.com/lifeandstyle/2019/jan/09/ constant-cravings-is-addiction-on-the-rise

15. Hari, J. (2016). *Chasing the scream: The inspiration for the feature film "The United States vs. Billie Holiday."* Bloomsbury USA. https://www.theguardian .com/books/2016/apr/12/johann-hari-chasing-the-scream-war-on-drugs

16. Salleh M. R. (2008). Life event, stress and illness. *Malaysian Journal of Medical Sciences,*15(4), 9–18.

17. Panchal, N., Kamal, R., Cox, C., & Garfield, R. (2021). The implications of COVID-19 for mental health and substance use. https://www.kff.org /coronavirus-covid-19/issue-brief/the-implications-of-covid-19-for-mental -health-and-substance-use

18. Panchal, N., Kamal, R., Cox, C., & Garfield, R. (2021). The implications of COVID-19 for mental health and substance use. https://www.kff.org/ coronavirus-covid-19/issue-brief/the-implications-of-covid-19-for-mental -health-and-substance-use

19. World Health Organization (2022). Suicide. https://www.who.int/news -room/fact-sheets/detail/suicide

20. Centers for Disease Control and Prevention (n.d.). Suicide is a leading cause of death in the United States. https://www.nimh.nih.gov/health/ statistics/suicide

21. Kumar, M. B., & Tjepkema, M. (2019, June 28). Suicide among First Nations people, Métis and Inuit (2011–2016): Findings from the 2011 Canadian Census Health and Environment Cohort (CanCHEC). https:// www150.statcan.gc.ca/n1/pub/99-011-x/99-011-x2019001-eng.htm

PART TWO: THE ROADMAP BACK TO EACH OTHER

CHAPTER SEVEN: ACKNOWLEDGMENT

1. Perry, B. D., & Winfrey, O. (2021). *What happened to you: Conversations on trauma, resilience, and healing.* Flatiron Books.

2. Korzinski, D. (2018, January 23). Half of Canadian adults say they don't have a will: Angus Reid Institute poll. Angus Reid Institute. https://angusreid .org/half-canadian-adults-say-dont-will-angus-reid-institute-poll

3. Government of Canada. Reducing the number of Indigenous children in care. https://www.sac-isc.gc.ca/eng/1541187352297/1541187392851

CHAPTER EIGHT: EMPATHY

1. Guthridge, M., & Giummarra, M. J. (2021). The taxonomy of empathy: A meta-definition and the nine dimensions of the empathic system. *Journal of Humanistic Psychology.* https://doi.org/10.1177/00221678211018015

2. Brown, B. (2021). *Atlas of the heart: Mapping meaningful connection and the language of human experience.* Random House.

3. Brown, B. (2021). *Atlas of the heart: Mapping meaningful connection and the language of human experience.* Random House.

4. Edlins, M., & Dolamore, S. (2018). Ready to serve the public? The role of empathy in public service education programs. *Journal of Public Affairs Education,* 24(3), 300–320.

5. Levett-Jones, T., & Cant, R. (2019). The empathy continuum: An evidenced-based teaching model derived from an integrative review of contemporary nursing literature. *Journal of Clinical Nursing,* 29(7–8), 1026–1040.

6. Wiseman, T. (1996). A concept analysis of empathy. *Journal of Advanced Nursing,* 23(6), 1162–1167. https://doi.org/10.1046/j.1365-2648.1996.12213.x

7. Brown, B. (2021). *Atlas of the heart: Mapping meaningful connection and the language of human experience.* Random House.

8. Fischer, A. H., Kret, M. E., & Broekens, J. (2018). Gender differences in emotion perception and self-reported emotional intelligence: A test of the emotion sensitivity hypothesis. *PloS one,* 13(1), e0190712. https://doi.org/10.1371/journal.pone.0190712

9. Chaplin, T. M., & Aldao, A. (2013). Gender differences in emotion expression in children: A meta-analytic review. *Psychological Bulletin,* 139(4), 735–765.

10. Deng, Y., Chang, L., Yang, M., Huo, M., & Zhou, R. (2016). Gender differences in emotional response: Inconsistency between experience and expressivity. *PLoS ONE,* 11(6).

11. Aron, A., Melinat, E., Aron, E. N., Vallone, R. D., & Bator, R. J. (1997). The experimental generation of interpersonal closeness: A procedure and some preliminary findings. *Personality and Social Psychology Bulletin*, 23(4), 363–377.

CHAPTER NINE: BE KIND AND DON'T TOLERATE BULLSHIT

1. Mathers, N. (2016). Compassion and the science of kindness: Harvard Davis Lecture 2015. *British Journal of General Practice*, 66(648), e525-e527. https://doi.org/10.3399/bjgp16X686041

2. Hart, D. (2021, February 11). Kindness: The glue that holds marriages together. https://www.frc.org/blog/2021/02/kindness-glue-holds-marriages-together

3. Mayo Clinic (2018–2021). The art of kindness. https://www.mayoclinic healthsystem.org/hometown-health/speaking-of-health/the-art-of-kindness#:~:text=Being%20kind%20boosts%20serotonin%20 and,ways%20you%20can%20create%20happiness

4. Wegenheim, J. (2022). Credits for kindness. https://www.gse.harvard.edu /news/ed/16/05/credits-kindness

5. Tiayon, S. B. (2020). How memories of kindness can make you happy. https://greatergood.berkeley.edu/article/item/how_memories_of _kindness_can_make_you_happy

6. Tawwab, N. G. (2021). *Set boundaries, find peace: A guide to reclaiming yourself*. TarcherPerigee

7. Covey, S. (2020). *The 7 habits of highly effective people*, 30th anniversary edition. Simon & Schuster.

PART THREE: WHEN WE LOSE OUR WAY AGAIN

1. Benbassat, N. (2020). Reflective function: A move to the level of concern. *Theory & Psychology*, 30(5), 657–673.

2. Steele, C. M., Spencer, S. J., & Aronson, J. (2002). Contending with group image: The psychology of stereotype and social identity threat. In M. P. Zanna (Ed.), *Advances in Experimental Social Psychology* (Vol. 34), pp. 379–440. Academic Press.

3. Fonagy, P., & Target, M. (2002). Early intervention and the development of self-regulation. *Psychoanalytic Inquiry*, 22(3), 307–335.

4. Batson, C. D., Lishner, D. A., Carpenter, A., Dulin, L., Harjusola-Webb, S., Stocks, E. L., Gale, S., Hassan, O., & Sampat, B. (2003). ". . . As you would have them do unto you": Does imagining yourself in the other's place stimulate moral action? *Personality & Social Psychology Bulletin*, 29(9), 1190–1201.

5. Wiseman, T. (1996). A concept analysis of empathy. *Journal of Advanced Nursing*, 23(6), 1162–1167.

6. Cassidy, K. W., Werner, R. S., Rourke, M., Zubernis, L. S., & Balaraman, G. (2003). The relationship between psychological understanding and positive social behaviors. *Social Development* (Oxford, England), 12(2), 198–221.

CHAPTER TEN: PRACTICE 1—YOUR PEOPLE

1. Albom, M. (2004). *Tuesdays with Morrie: An old man, a young man, and life's greatest lesson.* Random House.

2. Brown, B. (2017). *Rising strong: How the ability to reset transforms the way we live, love, parent, and lead.* Random House.

3. Carrington, J. (2019). *Kids these days: A game plan for (re)connection to those we teach, lead, and love.* Impress.

4. Bowlby, J. (1988). *A secure base: Parent-child attachment and healthy human development.* Tavistock professional book. Routledge.

5. Hoffman, K., Cooper, G., & Powell, B. (2017). *Raising a secure child: How circle of security parenting can help you nurture your child's attachment, emotional resilience, and freedom to explore.* Guilford Press.

CHAPTER ELEVEN: PRACTICE 2—DROP THOSE SHOULDERS

1. Renoir, T., Hasebe, K., & Gray, L. (2013). Mind and body: How the health of the body impacts on neuropsychiatry. *Frontiers in Pharmacology*, 158(4).

2. Keng, S. L., Smoski, M. J., & Robins, C. J. (2011). Effects of mindfulness on psychological health: A review of empirical studies. *Clinical Psychology Review*, 31(6), 1041–1056.

3. Bentzen, J. S. (2021). In crisis, we pray: Religiosity and the COVID-19 pandemic. *Journal of Economic Behavior & Organization*, 192, 541–583.

4. Behere, P. B., Das, A., Yadav, R., & Behere, A. P. (2013). Religion and mental health. *Indian Journal of Psychiatry*, 55(Suppl 2), S187–S194. (Retraction published *Indian J Psychiatry*, 2019 Jan; 61 [Suppl 3]: S632).

5. Mikołajczak, M., & Pietrzak, J. (2014). Ambivalent sexism and religion: Connected through values. *Sex Roles*, 70(9), 387–399.

6. Brown, B. (2013). *Daring greatly: How the courage to be vulnerable transforms the way we live, love, parent, and lead.* London: Portfolio Penguin.

7. Brown, B. (2018, November 21). Brené Brown on joy and gratitude. https://globalleadership.org/articles/leading-yourself/brene-brown-on-joy-and-gratitude

8. Brown, B. (2021). *Atlas of the heart: Mapping meaningful connection and the language of human experience.* Random House.

9. Allen, S. (2018). *The science of gratitude.* Greater Good Science Center: UC Berkeley.

10. Okura, L. (2017, December 6). Brené Brown: "Joy is the most vulnerable emotion we experience." https://www.huffpost.com/entry/brene-brown-joy-numbing-oprah_n_4116520

11. Seligman, M. E. P. (2002). *Authentic happiness: Using the new positive psychology to realize your potential for lasting fulfillment.* Free Press.

12. Thomas, P. A., Liu, H., & Umberson, D. (2017). Family relationships and well-being. *Innovation in Aging*, 1(3).

13. Janzen, J. (2020). *Bring the joy.* Fedd Books.

CHAPTER TWELVE: PRACTICE 3—BRINGING THE BIGGER PICTURE INTO FOCUS

1. Sinek, S. (2011). *Start with why: How great leaders inspire everyone to take action.* Portfolio.

2. Pink, D. H. (2022). *The power of regret: How looking backward moves us forward.* Riverhead.

3. David, S. (2016). *Emotional agility: Get unstuck, embrace change, and thrive in work and life.* Penguin Random House.

INDEX